Dr. G. ZANDER'S

MEDICO-MECHANICAL GYMNASTICS

ITS

METHOD, IMPORTANCE AND APPLICATION

BY

Dr. ALFRED LEVERTIN

FORMER ASSISTANT OF DR. G. ZANDER (1876—1885),
LECTURER ON BALNEOLOGY AT THE MEDICAL SCHOOL OF STOCKHOLM,
DIRECTOR OF THE MEDICO-MECHANICAL ZANDER INSTITUTE
AT ÖSTERMALM IN STOCKHOLM,
HEAD-PHYSICIAN AT THE BATHING ESTABLISHMENT OF VARBERG.

WITH A PORTRAIT OF DR. ZANDER,
SEVERAL EXPLANATORY ILLUSTRATIONS AND A MAP.

STOCKHOLM
P. A. NORSTEDT & SÖNER. PRINTERS TO THE KING.
1893

G. Zander

Respectfully and Gratefully

Dedicated

To

His highly appreciated
Teacher and Friend

Dr. Gustaf Zander

By

The Author.

PREFACE.

A work sprung from an urgent necessity and to which is devoted all one's energy; a scientific domain explored for years and the care of which has become one's mission; theories which in practice have been found good in so manifold ways, and yet are not sufficiently appreciated, — all this generally inspires an irrisistible desire to give utterance to one's convictions, in order to make accessible to others the results attained and the facts confirmed by many years' experience. The publishing of this present book in English must be attributed to a desire to lay before English physicians these facts and these results and to awaken in them a greater interest in our method of treatment. The future will show whether I have been successful in the difficult task of representing my subject in a sufficiently interesting manner to retain to the end the unwearied attention of my readers; although to have only partially attained this object would give me the greatest satisfaction.

As scarcely anything has been written in English on our method of treatment, I have conscientiously tried to collect from the best existing sources all that has been published on the subject in other languages, carefully avoiding even the appearance of partiality in examining and sifting the rich though scattered material, in the endeavour to point out all the most important and most characteristic parts of the respective works of the authors, although it would of course be a grave mistake to assume that these works do not contain much other instructive and interesting matter. This is particularly so in the case of our honoured friend, Dr. Nebel, whose arguments we so often quote. A medical man who devotes himself to a thorough study of our method, will soon recognise what a treasure his works are.

Thanks to this appreciated author, as well as to other colleagues who, with their influence, energy, knowledge of facts and true courage, plead the cause and importance of medical gymnastics, we have succeeded in having our method introduced into many foreign countries and especially Germany. The astonishing success of the Zander treatment gradually triumphs over the prejudice which generally opposes the introduction of the unknown. And so we have every reason to state with satisfaction that the Zander method of gymnastics gains ground day by day. Yet we are still distant from the object we have in view, — that bathing-places, as well as important cities, larger provincial towns and all Trades-Associations, [1] may found Zander gymnastic Institutes, with a well calculated attention to their own economical interest, and consequently to their own advantage as well as to the welfare of the sick and suffering No prophet's eyes are needed to behold now in spirit the time when the Medical Faculties of foreign countries will so highly appreciate the Zander method that it will be classed amongst other medical studies. In fact the Swedish medical gymnastics or kinesipathy, as they are also named, have a great future and a safe guarantee for rational treatment only in the hands of medical men.

The Zander gymnastic method is a popularisation of science; for, owing to the low price, it is accessible to all; rich and poor, high and low can profit in equal degree from its beneficial power. This Swedish invention may be considered as a universal good, not only by the simplicity of its means, but also by its efficiency; and whoever examines it without prejudice, will certainly enlist under its flag and work vigorously for its future.

It remains to give my warmest thanks to Dr. G. ZANDER and to Mr. E. GÖRANSSON C. E. for their obliging kindness in placing material and drawings at my disposal.

Stockholm, November 1893.

A. LEVERTIN, M. D.

___

[1] See Chapt. VIII.

The following work by my former assistant, Dr. A. Levertin, has for its object partly to give a review of all the literature to be found at present regarding my mechanical gymnastic treatment, partly also to give, by extracts from the works of several authors, a clear notion of the mission, the effects and the present development of this method of treatment. The author has also given many precious contributions from his own rich experience.

Having perused the manuscript of the work in question, I cannot but give Dr. Levertin my best thanks for the exertions he has made for the advancement of our cause, and I am convinced that, for the physicians who wish to obtain a general knowledge of the essence of mechanical gymnastics, as well as for those who desire to give themselves up to a profound study of our method, this book will prove a welcome introduction.

Stockholm, November 1893.

G. ZANDER.

Contents.

INTRODUCTION.

It is beyond all doubt that no previous century has equalled the 19th in scientific discoveries and researches. And this is true of Medical science more than of all others. Some 50 years ago we saw it governed by stereotyped theories, imprisoned in primitive forms which nobody ventured to touch, probably for fear of seeing the whole artificially supported building collapse, if the mystic pillars were touched. Nobody will dispute or misunderstand that biological and pathological researches have had the greatest results. These researches cannot but have exercised a powerful, and sovereign influence on therapeutics: the just appreciation of the process of life, the study of the morbid changes of the organism would naturally subject to a severe criticism the real worth of the therapeutic means inherited from an antiquated medical science, thus promoting the victory of truth for the benefit of mankind. We will not admit the results of this criticism within the scope of our treatise. We will rather turn our minds to the new curative methods at our service, methods representing great and important factors in the medical science of the future. They work perhaps as much for preventing the evil as for suppressing morbid symptoms which have already appeared. They have been called physical remedies; for they dispose of the powers of nature and use them as obedient tools at their service. Light, air, water, electricity and exercise are the names of these new remedies, each of which has put its stamp on the new therapeutics of the 19th century.

Our purpose here is to examine more closely *movement* as a therapeutic agent, and more especially the form of it which has been called mechanical gymnastics. In order to show its historical development and great importance as one of the

principal therapeutic agents of the future, and, by way of introduction to this work particularly intended for medical men,
we cannot do better than begin by a biographical sketch of
their inventor, Dr. GUSTAF ZANDER. We will even go back
a little further in order to show how it happened that in our
country, Sweden, the first attempt was made to render mechanical power subservient to therapeutics.

PER HENRIK LING had given the impulse and form for the
use of movement as a medical agent. His history, work and
success are so generally known that we can pass them here in
silence. By founding, in 1813, ›The Central gymnastic Institute› of Stockholm, he became the head of a school which still
exists and continues its successful work for the good of humanity, though on new, improved and more rational methods.
LING offers many unmistakable points of resemblance with
VINCENZ PRIESSNITZ, the founder of hydropathy. Neither belonged to the medical profession, but thanks to the genius with
which Providence had endowed them, they both prepared the way
for the new curative methods, hydropathy and medical gymnastics. It is however only in the hands of a professional that
these methods answer their purpose and obtain the appreciation
that their astonishing success justly deserves. When the mystical
additions, which at an earlier period surrounded medical gymnastics, had been removed by scientific researches and experiments, the fundamental truth of their ideas began to make
its way and is now gradually gaining ground. LING'S fanatical disciples, empirical like himself, adopted with eagerness
all the theories established by him. They were indeed incapable of examining critically the doctrines received, of separating
the pure metal from the dross, and they worked principally but
by the propaganda they knew so well how to make, for the admirable manual technics of LING'S method. Not one of his
disciples succeeded in making gymnastics progress one step in
theory. Besides, in Sweden, the native country of LING'S gymnastics, its promoters and the representatives of medical science
were in less friendly, if not althogether hostile relations to
each other. Against the school of LING and his fanatical disciples (GABRIEL BRANTING, AUGUSTUS GEORGII, PEHR JACOB
LIEDBECK etc.) there was the orthopedical school, principally

formed on French and German models, and represented first
by Professor NILS ÅKERMAN, and later by Dr. CARL HERMAN
SÄTHERBERG. Consequently, on one side was pure empiricism,
on the other theoretical science.

On many points SÄTHERBERG deviated from the pure and
exclusive orthopedy, and, as an auxiliary to the bandage-treatment, used medical gymnastic exercises, of which in many cases
he simplified and improved the method. His Institute became
the school where the representatives of medical science learned
to understand the utility and worth of gymnastic treatment.
We are quite willing to pass over the fierce conflicts which took
place between the said schools from the beginning to the middle
of the decade 1850—60, which can only be of interest in a history of Swedish gymnastics. It was not until the year 1864
that the post of Head Teacher (Professor) of the medical division at the Central Gymnastic Institute was given to a physician, Dr. TRULS JOHAN HARTELIUS, who remained at his post
until 1887, when he was succeeded by the present Professor,
Dr. ROBERT MURRAY.

A perfect calm succeeded these long and violent conflicts
and from that time the two schools worked together in harmony,
both benevolently supported from public funds. Swedish medical gymnastics had indeed to undergo many changes before
they became what they now are.

It is easy to understand that it was very hard work to give
movements on the Ling system. »How can you stand giving
such a number of movements?» a patient one day asked the
gymnast into whose hands he had entrusted himself. — ›I cannot stand it», was the reply. And so it was, for after some
time his health was irretrievably lost. This case shows sufficiently the dark side of the manual gymnastics. It is true
that forced work of this kind may not always bring on injurious consequences for the movement-giver, but the weariness
that a skilled and popular gymnast must feel after treating one
patient after another for many hours, will surely have a more
or less disadvantageous influence on the treatment of the patient. This fact is expressed by a writer in a foreign pe-
riodical in the following manner: »The gymnast is mistaken, if
he thinks that his weariness is the effect of increase of strength

in the patient, or that an occasional development of strength in himself corresponds to a passing weakness in the patient.» Whatever may be the advantages of the manual method in some respects, it is difficult to deny the truth of these words; for besides the inevitable weariness of the gymnast after several hours' work, he is also subjected to occasional influences which diminish his strength, and consequently the intensity of the movements cannot always be the same.

How are these inconveniences to be avoided? Is it possible to find a remedy for the evil? Yes, but only in case there could be found a movement-giver insured against weariness and indisposition, who could with minute exactness increase or diminish the degree of resistance according to the prescriptions of the physicians, and who knew how to adapt himself to the varying strength of the patient. This problem has been solved for the first time by Dr. GUSTAF ZANDER by means of his remarkable gymnastic apparatus. Already as a young student he had conceived the plan of his renowned system. He was then conducting the gymnastic exercises at a Ladies' boarding-school established by his sisters at Bårarp (Halland, Sweden). This is what he himself relates on the subject:

»In 1857 I made the first attempt at creating a complete system of gymnastics by means of mechanical apparatus at a boarding-school for girls in the country. I tried gymnastics with LING'S apparatus as well as free exercises, i. e. gymnastics without apparatus. But I was obliged to reject both: the former because it did not very well suit girls, the latter because it did not allow the variety and the necessary individualisation of movements for sickly girls, and especially for those suffering from curvatures of the spine. There was no way left but for me to give by the manual method some medical gymnastic exercises, more or less modified. The insufficiency of my strength gave me the idea to substitute it by mechanical agents. Besides I hoped to avoid by this means some other inconveniences of the manual method which I had had an opportunity of ascertaining both as patient and gymnast. Then I set myself the following question to solve:

»If a mechanical apparatus could be invented which compelled the activity of a certain group of muscles to set it in motion, and if it were possible to furnish this apparatus with a balance-weight which could be increased and diminished at will, in conformity with the laws according to which the muscular strength works, the problem might be considered solved, and an agent would be obtained which not only substituted the gymnast, but would also be able to triumph over difficulties against which *he* struggled in vain. Apparatus for the most important movements were manufactured on this plan by way of experiment, and though these first apparatus were most primitive and imperfect, I was not disappointed in my hopes. I was able to individualise the movements, and after some experiments could exactly determine the degree of effort suitable for each pupil on beginning the exercises, and then slowly and imperceptibly increase the resistance. The sure and regular increase of strength resulting from this treatment was really astonishing. Within a very short time even the most delicate among the girls made progress, easily ascertained by the increase of strength indicated on the scale of resistance, as well as by improved appetite and greater moral and physical vigour».

It was not until the year 1862 however, after the school had been removed from Bårarp to Partilled (Vestergötland), where the premises were spacious enough for a gymnasium, that Dr. Zander began to construct and develop his apparatus and his method systematically. He was then only 27 years old. Zander did not, like most modern inventors, from his childhood show special aptitude for mechanics, but this long felt want in medicine suddenly brought to light the latent powers of the young man. He had never devoted himself to any special study of mechanics, and yet, in solving the appointed problem, he succeeded even to the minutest details. In his first attempts he had no other assistance than that of a village blacksmith and a carpenter; but within him burnt the fire of innate genius and the love for his science possessed by a genuine physician. Precisely because he was in the beginning reduced to narrow means, he acquired a mechanical ingenuity which has often excited the astonishment and admiration of experienced mechanicians.

ZANDER considered the continuation and improvement of this branch of gymnastics his mission. Already in the year 1864

he was able to lay before the Medical Faculty of Stockholm a
dissertation on his gymnastic method. This dissertation, written
for his degree of Licentiate, won him a first class certificate
with honours. At the meeting of the Swedish Doctors of Medicine, Dec. 20th 1864, Dr. ZANDER invited the members then
present to examine and test the mechanical apparatus invented
by him with the object of substituting manual treatment in medical gymnastics. In January of the following year Dr. Zander was able to open to the public his Medico-mechanical Institute which did not then possess more then 27 apparatus. The
inventive genius of ZANDER, however, never rested; indefatigably
working for his great object, he has always been creating
something new, so that at the present moment the Institute possesses 71 different gymnastic and orthopedic apparatus.

It is scarcely needful to say that Dr. ZANDER had to conquer much opposition before he succeeded in realising his ideas.
The following is what a highly esteemed writer on this subject,
Dr. EMIL KLEEN,[1] says concerning the matter: »By using steam-
power in the mechanical therapeutics, Dr. ZANDER caused a
storm of displeasure to break out on all sides, most vividly re-
minding one of similar manifestations wherever steam-power
was introduced to supplant manual work, a proceeding against
which violated interests declaimed as loudly as possible. This
man of genius with his serious intentions and vast medical
knowledge was exposed to odious attacks and placed in the
same category as notorious quacks by persons who knew neither
him nor his apparatus.»

These struggles were not of long duration, however, and
in our country both the Zander method and the manual method
have in the medical world and among the public most zealous
defenders and zealous partisans who consider the method of
their choice the only way to salvation. As early as the year
1873 Professor HARTELIUS gave, in the medical review »Hygiea»
(vol. XXXV p. 318), a description of the different gymnastic
methods in an evidently conciliatory manner. »This description
of the manual and mechanical methods of medical gymnastics», said Dr. HARTELIUS, »has simply for object to represent

[1] Manual of massage by Dr. EMIL KLEEN, translated from Swedish
into German by Dr. G. Schütz, Berlin 1890, (Page 25).

15

both of them in their true light and exact relation to each
other, and not to exaggerate our praise of the one at the expense
of the other. May they both display their advantages! May there
be competition between them or, rather, may they mutually complete one another — each in its proper sphere. As for us, we
consider it a desirable thing that the mechanical method might
substitute the manual one, for it would be an advantage to humanity.» — The Medical Faculty of Upsala gave Dr. ZANDER
a great testimony of its appreciation by making him Honorary
Doctor on the occasion of the great 400-years' jubilee of the
University of Upsala in 1877. In 1880 he was appointed »Do-
cent» or Lecturer on Medical Gymnastics at the Medical School
of Stockholm, with the right of giving instruction in his method.
That was undoubtedly an immense step forward for medical
gymnastics whose existence by the side of other branches of
medical science was thereby recognised after a long struggle.
The apparatus constructed by Dr. ZANDER for trunk-measuring, certainly the best of our days, was epoch-making as a
proof of the justness of his treatment in a special branch of
medical gymnastics. »Thanks to this apparatus», said he one
day to the writer of this sketch, »I first succeeded in getting at
the essence and nature of the treacherous disease called scoliosis or lateral curvature of the spine. By means of my
measuring-apparatus I shall be able hereafter to prove mathe-
matically the efficiency of my curative method. It has given
and ever gives me an incentive to further invention of orthopedic apparatus. As long as I was exclusively guided by my
eyes and my mechanical notions, I had to grope in the dark.
Hereafter I shall be able to prove incontestably by graphic re-
presentation the results I obtain by means of my treatment.
    Dr. ZANDER has exhibited to the Society of Swedish Doc-
tors of Medicine as well as to the general Medical Congress
at Upsala his apparatus for trunk-measuring and found great
appreciation; his system in general has been an object of warm
eulogy in foreign special reviews.
    We cannot better conclude this biographical sketch than by
quoting words spoken concerning Dr. ZANDER on the occasion
of the 15th anniversary of the Medico-mechanical Institute:
»Here in Stockholm the docile power of steam puts in motion

a great number of apparatus, worked with the purpose of strengthening a weak and languishing body; but the real motive power is this modest, unpretending man with a dreamy countenance and honest blue eyes, where the benevolent expression is the reflection from a heart, which in the solution of scientific problems has always tended towards the noble aim: relief to human suffering.»

GUSTAF ZANDER was born in Stockholm, March 29th 1835. His father was »Rådman» (member of the Court of 1st instance) J. G. ZANDER, his mother MARGARET VILHELMINE BECKSTEDT. ZANDER, first attended the College of St. Clara and then the Lyceum of Stockholm, went to Upsala in 1855, took his first medical degree in 1856, his second in 1860, and his degree of Licentiate of medicine in Stockholm in 1864. He was made Knight of the Swedish Order of the North-Star in 1875, immediately after the first visit paid by His Majesty to the gymnasium, and as an expression of the Royal appreciation of the Zander method. The following year he obtained a government-allowance for the purpose of visiting the Universal Exhibition at Philadelphia where his method was awarded a prize-medal, as was also the case at Brussels (1876) and at the Universal Exhibition of Paris in 1878. In 1892 the Society of Swedish Physicians gave him its semi-centennial gold-medal. Dr. Zander is married to FANNY AGNES ELEONOR HANSEN, native of Lübeck. Eight children are the issue of this marriage.

The Theory of the Zander method.

Leaving totally aside in this treatise the manual method, we will exclusively occupy ourselves with medico-mechanical gymnastics, and try to group the principal points that their founder Dr. ZANDER, as well as other writers, has specially emphasised of the nature and indications of the said method.

By way of introduction we will quote a German writer[1] who insists on that very motive which led us to collect into a whole the scattered material contained in divers reviews, programmes and papers:

»The object of the following lines is to propagate the Zander method in medical and non-medical circles, to show the attention and appreciation which it deserves in the highest degree. I will further clearly lay before the public various views of the authors, refute errors, fight opposition by a thorough examination of works already published, and also, by my own practical studies contribute to the propagation of the method, thereby honouring to the best of my ability Dr ZANDER'S successful invention.» — »No branch of medical science and its application», he says elsewhere,[2] »has been so much neglected, even by great physicians, as the mechanical gymnastics. Last spring, for instance, one of the most celebrated physicians of Berlin was called to a consultation concerning a person suffering from heart-disease, and when the physician who usually attended the patient, alluded to the astonishing success of the

---

[1] A. KÜHNER, Gesundheit. Zeitschrift für öffentliche und private Hygiene, Jahrgang XVI, n:o 9, Seite 131.

[2] Blätter für Klinische Hydrotheraphie. Jahrgang I, s. 119.

mechanical method of treatment, the professor, who was totally ignorant of the Medico-Mechanical Institute and its method, answered: »I would not advise you to try such bold experiments!» Often the Zander method is known only by name to practising physicians. The medical-scientific world has entirely neglected this method, the practising of which is indeed more complex, takes infinitely more time and is less remunerative than written prescriptions. A great number of physicians think and speak like the anti-conservative member who once said in Parliament: »I certainly do not know the intentions of the Government, but I disapprove of them.»

Dr. KÜHNER further quotes the following from Dr. KLEEN'S work: »If ZANDER has had the misfortune of being misjudged by some practitioners of gymnastics, he has however, had the inestimable good fortune of finding in Dr. NEBEL a perfectly disinterested advocate, distinguished by his great ability, and without whom his method would scarcely have attained its present dimensions.»

Dr. NEBEL has related the results of his rich experience in a work that we most warmly recommend to the practising phycician, and the importance of which is all the greater that ZANDER has given to every part of the book contributions from his own vast experience, has examined and sifted all its details and has so well guided his young collaborator, that, without fear of being mistaken, we may call this work the most important motor that we possess for the dissemination and scientific appreciation of our method in the medical world. NEBEL has not, however, in any way sacrificed his indepedence as a scientific explorer. He has employed the material received as from precious sources, and, thus guided, he has succeeded in finding his way in the »terra incognita» of gymnastics, as well as in throwing new light on the subject. To make this circumstance understood as it deserves to be, we take the liberty of quoting the following lines from his work: [1]

»Again and again I have had to quote Dr. ZANDER'S own words, either from his shorter publications or, and principally, from a series of letters in which he answers my questions on

---

[1] Bewegungslehre mittelst Schwedischer Gymnastik etc. von Dr. H. NEBEL. Frankfurt a/M. P. 61.

his ideas and his method òf treatment, giving me good and useful advice. These documents which are of very great value to me, testify as much to the great amiability as to the mature reflection of the learned man. Dr. ZANDER has a right to demand and expect a more serious examination and appreciation of his method than has yet been bestowed on it in our country.»

In order to characterise the work of NEBEL may we be permitted to repeat the last lines of our criticism of it in a Swedish review at the time: ›We hail with pleasure this important work of the author, and as a Swede, I thank him specially for all he is doing and has done to show the medical world what an important factor we, Swedes, have found in medical gymnastics for the work of modern scientific culture.»

Those of our readers who know more intimately the Zander apparatus and follow with interest the reports of results obtained by their means, will be obliged to acknowledge that these apparatus are the result of diligent study, the outcome of a work of many years, of days and nights spent in toilsome researches. It is only after many attempts that these apparatus have obtained the perfection of form which allows their use in the service of science and of suffering humanity. How perfectly justified are we not therefore in branding with infamy the clumsy attempts of those who, led by mercenary motives, bring into the market defective apparatus which by their insufficiency cannot in any way answer the desired purpose.

Some well-intentioned physicians may wish, no doubt, to add to the number of their medical gymnastic apparatus, and, with the Zander apparatus before them, they are led to attempt the construction of similar ones. But — »nemo nascitur artifex» says an ancient proverb, and no physician is capable of becoming a mechanico-therapeutical constructor, unless he has, like Zander, passed through all the degrees of science and practice. It is not sufficient to be able to give glimpses and hints to a practical mechanician on the exigencies of medicine, one must also oneself be capable of constructing, and of giving visible form to the medical thought. Dr. KÜHNER whom we have quoted already in the preceding pages, and whom we shall have occasion to quote again in support of our statements, expresses on this subject, in a German review, the following excellent ideas:

»Everywhere, practising physicians have to struggle against quackery. With respect to the Zander method we have reason to add the important circumstance that there exist many pompous imitations of the original Zander apparatus, and the cheaply acquired title of »Director», »Professor» makes even physicians believe that it is a question of scientific mechanico-therapeutics. There exist indeed so-called medico-mechanical institutes, *not* directed by physicians, which institutes are using some imitations of Zander apparatus and other apparatus for various forms of exercise and, by laymen and sometimes even by physicians, these institutes are taken for real Zander Institutes, i. e. scientifically directed institutes, furnished with *genuine* Zander apparatus.

Those who visited the medical congress of Wiesbaden, held in the spring of the year 1891 might have seen in a hall next to that of the Hygienic Exhibition a number of designs rather good and not without »réclame» concerning a so-called medico-mechanical Institute analogous with that of Baden-Baden. It is an establishment however, which has nothing in common with the Zander Institute of Baden-Baden but the usurped name, and it does not in any way answer the demands which can be made upon a Zander Institute.

However clear and evident all this may seem to the eyes of those initiated in the essence of gymnastics, one who, for the first time, gives himself to these general considerations, will have some difficulty in comprehending fully what we say here concerning the Zander method. We will therefore review and discuss certain questions which constitute essential parts and fundamental truths established by Dr. ZANDER. Let us listen to what NEBEL [1] says, speaking of the Swedish inventor:

»Consequently he constructed apparatus allowing the regulation of the resistance, so that it increases and diminishes gradually, according to the laws of levers and those governing the exercise of muscular power. The fact that this important advantage of the Zander method has been totally neglected in the NYCANDER apparatus, as well as in the PAZ system, is often forgotten.»

[1] Page 7.

Nobody has explained more clearly than ZANDER the influence of the laws for the lever on the movement of the muscles. Let us hear his own words:

›The muscles act principally on levers (the bones). But the force applied on a lever exercises a perceptibly different effect, according as the lever describes a right angle with the direction-line of the force, in which case the force acts strongest, or as it forms with the direction-line of the force an acute or obtuse angle, in which cases the force acts stronger, the less acute or the less obtuse the angle is, i. e. the more it approaches the right angle. The resistance in a gymnastic exercise ought therefore to be based on these rules. If not, the muscle would have too little work to execute when it acts most powerfully, and too little when it acts most feebly. That is exactly what easily happens in manual gymnastics. In mechanical gymnastics, on the contrary, the resistance is attached to a lever, and this lever accords as nearly as possible with the natural levers (the arm, the leg).

›For this reason the lever of the apparatus always develops its greatest resistance when the lever of the body (the arm, the leg) allows the greatest effect of the muscular power. Let us take for instance the apparatus A 9, *Forearm-flexion*. The resistance begins feebly and increases constantly till the arm and forearm form a right angle. The power of the muscle is then at its maximum, as well as the resistance. When the forearm begins to form an acute angle with the arm, the muscular power diminishes more and more and with it the resistance. How a power is modified by the levers is described in MEYER'S work: ›*Statics and mechanism of the human skeleton*›; it is simply a question of drawing, in each special case, a parallelogram of the powers in order to overcome all difficulties. So far the effect of the laws of the lever on muscular power.

›We must, however, pay attention to another circumstance, namely, *that the absolute power of the muscle is diminished the more it is contracted* (SCHWANN). Towards the end of the movement the patient can indeed give stronger contractive impulses to the working muscle and consequently overcome the increased resistance. Such a medical gymnastic exercise would, however, be incorrect.

»The difficulty is to give, in constructing the apparatus, a just influence to the laws of the lever, as well as to the rules given by SCHWANN. This cannot be effected by calculations only, for practical experiments are indispensable. Therefore, in the apparatus B 9, *Knee-flexion*, I have not placed the greatest resistance at the point where the thigh and the leg form a right angle, as the law of the lever would require, but *about 30° from this position*, as one can distinctly feel during the movement that the maximum of resistance is most easily overcome at this point.»

Here we have the outline of the fundamental law which enables us to explain the principles of our apparatus and to prove them practically even to the least experienced.

Never, therefore, have we shown our apparatus to interested visitors without drawing their attention to these laws, for it is principally in the construction of the apparatus for active movements that ZANDER'S inventive genius appears in all its strength and clearness, and it is in this construction that we recognise the considerable superiority of his apparatus to all others of the kind. The »passive apparatus» on the contrary, whatever be the ingenuity of their invention and construction, can never be measured with the active apparatus, when the question is to show in a clear and simple manner the possibility of substituting for the human hand a surer and, especially, more scientific agent. Still even the »passive apparatus» have, by their continuity and uniformity, a great advantage when compared with manual movements.

If a person, on first visiting one of our Institutes, considers the matter from the above mentioned point of view, his eyes will be opened, prejudices he might have had will disappear at once, and he will assuredly become a warm partisan of the Zander method. If, on the contrary, the visitor is first conducted to the apparatus for chest-expansion, for equitation, or to the vibration- and kneading-apparatus, he will admire all these fine things, like an honest rustic, who beholds for the first time some figures moved by concealed machinery. Without understanding these apparatus he will examine them with surprise, and the impression left will be the one we experience at the sight of some curiosity. But — if one takes the trouble to

explain simply, and within reach of the comprehension of the
visitor, these fundamental laws of our method, a great interest
in our cause and our system is generally roused, while we
rarely succeed in doing so by showing the wonderfully working
passive apparatus.

By thus proceeding it would further be impossible to fancy
a case of which we have heard, namely, that a celebrated physician believed for many years that our movements were exclusively passive i. e. that they were given only by means of the
motor, and that we bend and stretch joints and muscles by
using mechanical force. He was quite ignorant that our chief
strength consists in the fact that in our treatment the muscles
have to overcome a resistance equivalent to their power, and
that we are able to determine and portion out this resistance
down to its minutest and most delicate details — we will say
with as much precision and conscientious exactness as the medical doses by scruples and grains. That is the reason why
we always speak of the *apparatus* and not of the *machines*
of the Zander Gymnastics, for the latter name gives, to persons
ignorant of our method, incorrect notions and false ideas that
cause perfectly ridiculous attacks to be aimed at it.

Dr. ZANDER has further explained these questions in his
work: *The apparatus for medical gymnastic treatment and their
use,* [1] written in German. He says as follows:

»Experience has shown that regular muscular exercises with
progressive exertion, do not only develop and strengthen the
muscles, but also remove morbid changes in the tissues,
strengthen the nervous system and accelerate the circulation
of the blood and lymph, as well as the functions of a great
many organs. The introduction of these exercises among the
auxiliaries to health therefore was self-evident.

»It was necessary, however, to base these exercises on physiological laws, and to be able, as with other therapeutic means,
to modify their effects according to individual cases.

»From the year 1857, when I began to occupy myself with
medical gymnastics, I have been trying to meet these requirements by my mechanical gymnastic method and I have shown

---

[1] Die Apparate für mechanisch-heilgymnastische Behandlung und deren
Anwendung. 4. vermehrte Auflage. Stockholm 1893.

in several publications that the object could only be obtained, if the resistance to be overcome by the muscles is produced by means of mechanical apparatus and levers.

»The object of the use of levers is: 1:o, that the resistance is in the strictest accordance with the physiological and mechanical laws for the action of the muscles; and 2:o, that the application of the remedy is effected in the most perfect manner.

»I am not ignorant of the fact that at a comparatively recent date, and perhaps also before my time, several persons have constructed single apparatus for medical gymnastics. Still no one hitherto but myself, has constructed a complete series of apparatus for the harmonious development of the whole muscular system, or indicated the principles according to which the lever should be used in each separate apparatus.

»Therefore, if there exist to-day a *method of mechanical gymnastics*, it is mine.

»As already stated, the mechanical gymnastic method makes use of mechanical apparatus, a special one for the exercise of each separate group of muscles. The resistance to be overcome is obtained by the effect of the alternate contraction and relaxation of the muscle, whereby a weight attached to a lever is alternately raised and lowered. By the lever the important requirement is met that, *in the course of the movement, the resistance increases and diminishes with the natural changes in the mechanical effect of the muscular action.* When this effect is greatest, the lever assumes the position in which it reaches its greatest momentum, i. e. the horizontal; when the effect diminishes, the lever leaves this position; and when again the effect increases, the lever once more approaches the horizontal position.

»The weight can be moved along the lever and can be fastened by means of a screw at a greater or smaller distance from the fulcrum of the lever, so that every degree of weight desired, from zero to the maximum appropriate to each apparatus, can be easily obtained.

»Furnished with such apparatus the mechanical gymnastic method offers the following advantages:

1. During the movement the resistance adapts itself exactly to the natural changes in the effect of the muscular power.

2. The intensity of the movement is weighed, as in scales, and its exact degree can be measured.

3. The *gradual* increase of strength in the movement, so necessary for muscular development, can be accurately made and to any degree desired.

4. The resistance indicated by a given number is always the same and therefore any necessary regulation of the strength of the movement, whether increase or decrease, can be made easily and with precision.

Besides the muscular exercises which are the essence of all gymnastics, my mechanical gymnastic method also makes use of *passive* movements for the articulations, such as arm-rolling, foot-rolling, and of *mechanical operations:* vibrations, percussions, kneadings &c. &c.»

The Institutes where Dr. Zander's method of mechanical gymnastics is applied, are generally called *Medico-Mechanical Zander Institutes.* The first was founded in Stockholm in 1865. From the year of the opening of this Institute, the gymnastic establishments of Sweden began to employ his apparatus and since 1875 several Institutes of the kind have been founded in Sweden as well as abroad.

There are at present fully equipped Medico-mechanical Institutes in the following towns:

Stockholm, Gothenburg, Kristiania, Helsingfors, St. Petersburg, Baden-Baden, Hamburg, Berlin, Breslau, Mannheim, Frankfort-on-the-Main, Dresden, Würzburg, Leipzic, Wildbad, Stuttgart, Wiesbaden, Aix-la-Chapelle, Ragatz, London, Buenos-Ayres, New-York.

There are partially equipped Institutes in Stockholm, Upsala, Örebro, Norrköping, Hjulsta, Åbo, Moscow, Copenhagen, Karlsruhe, Pforzheim, Nieder-Schönhausen near Berlin, Munich, Elberfeld, Bochum, Königshütte, Chemnitz, Essen, Neu-Rahnsdorf near Berlin, Groningen, Vienna, Budapest, Turin, Baltimore, St. Louis.

Single apparatus for private use have been sent to Riga, Erfurt, Barmen, Trier, Berchtesgaden, Meiningen, Barcelona, Milan, Nicolajeff and Alexandria.

26

At present there exist in Stockholm two Institutes with complete equipment and two with a partial equipment of apparatus, of which latter Institutes, one is established by Dr. Zander for special treatment of scoliotic girls.

At Baden-Baden the advantages of the Zander method are recognized to such a degree that the Government of Baden has lately established a second complete Zander Institute. In addition, apparatus for complete Institutes are ordered for Boston and St. Francisco.

II.

The apparatus of the Medico-Mechanical Zander Gymnastics.

The apparatus for mechanical gymnastic treatment are divided into the three following series, according as they are set in motion, or have to operate only by pressure (*corrective pressure*).

First series: Apparatus set in motion by the muscular power of the patient.

Second series: Apparatus set in motion by means of some motor (steam-, gas- or electric-engine).

Third series: Apparatus exercising, by the weight of the patient's body or by mechanical arrangements, a *corrective pressure* on the frame, or producing the *tension* of elastic parts.

These apparatus are further divided into the following series according to the nature of their physiological effects.

I. Apparatus for active movements.
A. *Active movements of the arms.*

A 1. Arm-sinking.
A 2. Arm-raising.
A 3. Arm-pulling-downwards.
A 4. Arm-stretching-upwards.
A 5. Arm-adduction.

A 6. Arm-abduction.
A 7. Arm-rolling (circumduction).
A 8 a. Arm-rotation (active).
A 8 b. Arm-rotation (active-passive).
A 9. Forearm-flexion.
A 10. Forearm-extension.
A 11. Hand-flexion and extension.
A 12. Finger-flexion and extension.

B. *Active movements of the legs.*

B 1. Hip-flexion.
B 2. Hip-extension.
B 3. Hip-knee-flexion.
B 4. Hip-knee-extension.
B 5 a. Leg-adduction (sitting).
B 5 b. Leg-adduction (half-reclining).
B 6. Leg-abduction.
B 7. Velocipede-motion.
B 8. Leg-rotation.
B 9. Knee-flexion.
B 10. Knee-extension.
B 11. Foot-flexion and extension.
B 12. Foot-rolling.

C. *Active movements of the trunk.*

C 1. Trunk-flexion (sitting).
C 2. Trunk-extension (sitting).
C 3. Trunk-raising and flexion.
C 4. Trunk-extension (long-sitting).
C 5. Trunk-extension (standing).
C 6. Trunk-sideways-flexion.
C 7. Trunk-rotation.
C 8. Pelvis-turning.
C 10. Neck-extension.

D. *Balancing movements.*

D 1. Trunk-balancing.
D 2. Trunk-rolling (transversal sitting).
D 3. Trunk-rolling (saddle-sitting).

II. Apparatus for passive movements.

E. *Passive movements.*

E 2. Hand-flexion and extension (passive).
E 3. Hand-adduction and abduction (passive).
E 4. Finger-flexion and extension (passive).
E 6. Chest-expansion.
E 7. Trunk-rotation (passive).
E 8. Pelvis-elevation.

III. Apparatus for mechanical operations.

F. *Vibratory operations.*

F 1. Vibration (of different parts of the body).
F 2. Vibration, saddle-sitting (of the whole body).

G. *Percutient operations.*

G 1. Percussion (of different parts of the body).
G 3. Leg-percussion.
G 4. Trunk-percussion.
G 5. Head-percussion.

H. *Kneading operations.*

H 1. Abdomen-kneading.

I. *Rubbing operations.*

J 1. Arm-rubbing.
J 2 b. Finger-massage.
J 3. Leg-rubbing.
J 4. Foot-rubbing.
J 5. Back-rubbing.
J 6. Circular abdomen-rubbing.

IV. Orthopedic apparatus.

K. *Passive redressings.*

K 1. Lateral suspension (reclining).
K 2. Lateral pressure (lying).
K 3. Chest-rotation.
K 4. Redressing of lumbar scoliosis (sitting).
K 5. Lateral pressure (sitting).

L. *Active redressings.*

L 1. Combination of A 3 and D 1.
L 2. Strengthening of the lumbar region (lying).
L 3. Carrying the pelvis sideways.
L 4. Carrying the pelvis forwards-backwards.
L 5. Lateral flexion of the lumbar spine.
L 6. Straightening of the spine.

In addition to the above, Dr. ZANDER has invented three measuring apparatus, most important complements to the orthopedic apparatus, namely:

Measuring apparatus.

Trunk-measuring.
Cross-cut-measuring.
Examining-chair for scoliosis.

We add here the *General Rules for the use of the apparatus* given by Dr. ZANDER.

The movements which must be taken in the order indicated on the prescription, are divided into groups of three movements each. As a rule it is the first movement of the group which requires the greatest effort, i. e. an active arm- or trunk-movement. Then follows an active leg-movement and, at last, a passive movement or one of the mechanical operations. For more robust persons, however, more energetic movements can be combined in the same group; in that case the third movement can be either a balancing-movement or an active trunk-movement. The three movements of each group are taken immediately after each other, and then the patient should rest about 5 minutes, unless rest be prescribed after each movement.

In the beginning, all the movements should be slight. Even should the patient consider them insufficient, their strength should not be increased during the first days. In fact, even if each separate movement seems too slight in comparison to what he believes himself able to support, all the movements together require a considerable degree of activity, not only of the muscles, but also of the nerves, and greater fatigue is felt, especially towards evening, than was expected. Gymnastic movements have an infinitely greater effect than the ordinary, chiefly automatic, movements of daily life.

On the prescription is indicated by approximate estimation, the degree of force that the physician deems suitable for the patient. The instructor, who has supervision while the movements are taken, is free, however, to diminish the strength, if they are too strong, but he should take care not to increase it too soon. For the first day or days all the groups should not be attempted, at least not with delicate persons.

After a few days, when the first weariness has passed away, or if none has been felt, the intensity of the movements can be increased one degree at a time, until some slight fatigue is noticed. Then this degree of effort is maintained, until the weariness is entirely overcome, when the resistance is further increased. These precautions taken, the strength of the patient increases slowly but surely.

From what has been said, it is obvious that all fatigue is not to be anxiously avoided. Exertion, up to a certain degree, is an indispensable condition for increase of strength. As, however, a large number of persons using medical gymnas-tics are obliged, during the period of treatment, to go on with their ordinary occupations, which alone cause weariness, the strength of such patients should be carefully economised if they are to make progress. Hence the strict rule, not to use greater intensity of movement than to cause but a slight and quickly passing weariness.

There is no doubt, that with patients who are able to give themselves up entirely to the gymnastic treatment, and to un-dergo it two or three times daily with sufficient interval of rest, more speedy and complete results are obtained than is generally the case in medical gymnastic Institutes.

There are patients whose weariness is persistent, even though they have only a few slight movements. That is, however, no reason for losing courage. In some particular cases, the fatigue has lasted weeks and even months, before it has gradually passed away, giving place to an amazingly rapid increase of strength and general health. This form of weariness is a nervous affection due to a great many weakening influences, but principally to an enervating mode of life and a careful avoidance of all physi-cal exertion, except perhaps dancing and late hours. Absolute rest, if such were possible, might improve this state, but medi-cal gymnastics alone can restore health and strength to such patients. In that case they should of course submit themselves exclusively to gymnastic treatment. Unfortunately such patients are often induced by their persistent weariness to abandon the treatment too soon.

The prescription is methodically composed according to the needs and condition of patient. Therefore no change in the sequence of the movements should be made without consulting the physician. Those who use gymnastics whithout suffering from any particular disease, only for the purpose of main-taining health and strength, should keep to the order prescribed within each group, but they may alter the sequence of the groups. To gain time, movements of one group may be exchanged for similar ones of another group, as for instance, arm-, leg- and trunk-movements.

Any arbitrary modification of the movements in the prescription would, on the contrary, be out of the question, and certainly not tolerated.

The treatment intended to strengthen the constitution in general, by exercising and developing all the muscles, forms, as it were, the basis of the prescription. This treatment is afterwards modified and developed in such a way, that the movements calculated to affect some special ailment or disease become predominant by their repetition. Insight and experience are required for making and carrying out such a plan of treatment, besides the careful consideration of such modifications as occasional circumstances may render necessary. That is exactly what many people do not seem to understand. They omit movements which are not agreeable to them, or of which they do not see the use, and take others not prescribed which they prefer and which seem to them more suitable, perhaps because they bring into activity stronger and more exercised muscles. It is natural that these movements should *seem* agreeable and beneficial, while work with feeble and unexercised muscles is tiring and disagreable. However, the more the strong muscles are exercised at the expense of the weak ones, the more the organism degenerates, becomes unfit for its natural functions, and loses its power of resistance against unhealthy influences. The object of gymnastics is not attained, and the patient ascribes the failure to the method, instead of attributing it to his own unreasonable self-will.

A deep and regular respiration is of the greatest importance in gymnastics. The rhythm of the movements should coincide with the normal rhythm of the respiration, or that which most easily allows the production of deep inspirations and expirations. Deep inspirations are, however, rather troublesome to weak persons, or such as are not accustomed to bodily exercise. But, each active movement has two successive phases, one requiring greater effort (when the muscles contract and the lever of the apparatus is raised), and the other less effort (when the muscles relax and the lever sinks). That is the reason why I have found it suitable to make the expiration coin-

cide with the phase requiring greater effort and the inspiration
with that requiring less.

Exceptions to this rule are the movements in which the thorax
assumes the position of inspiration during the phase of greater
effort, such as A 2, A 4, A 6, C 2, C 4, C 5, C 10, and, for a special reason, also C 6 (see description of this movement).

Among the other movements we must distinguish those in
which the respiratory muscles take part and which consequently
make the rule given above indispensable, (expiration during the
phase requiring greater effort). There are also movements in which
the patient finds inspiration more convenient during the phase
requiring greater effort, chiefly because then the pause which
follows expiration in regular breathing coincides with that which
takes place before each repetition of the movements.

From what has been said it follows, that with respect to
the rules for respiration, the active movements are generally divided into four categories, namely:

1. *Movements in which the inspiration should be made
during the first phase, requiring the greater effort:* A 2, A 4,
A 6, C 2, C 4, C 5, C 6, C 10.

2. *Movements in which the inspiration precedes and the
movement begins at the following expiration, and in which consequently the expiration should be made during the phase requiring greater effort:* A 1, A 3, C 1, C 3, C 7 and C 8.

3. *Movements in which the patient breathes at will during
the first phase:* A 5, A 8 a, A 9, A 10, A 11, A 12, *as well as all
the leg-movements* except B 7, B 11 and B 12.

4. *Movements with respect to which the only prescription
necessary is a deep and calm respiration:* A 7, A 8 b, B 7, B 11,
B 12, D 1, D 2, D 3, *and in passive movements and mechanical
operations.*

It is a matter of course that all the movements should be
executed quietly and regularly.

Other rules to be observed:

Patients should reach the Institute in time to take the prescribed movements quietly and with sufficient intervals of rest.

They should not fatigue themselves before or after the exercise, which rule must be particularly observed by patients suffering from heart-disease, and from general weakness

The physician should be informed if, nevertheless, marked or continued weariness follows the exercise.

The whole attention should be given to the exercise, and there should be neither conversation nor reading while it lasts.

Dancing and late hours should be avoided during treatment for general weakness.

Loose, comfortable clothing should be worn, leaving waist and throat free, the breathing and the use of the arms unimpeded and the abdominal organs without pressure. Stays, tight neckties and garters should be avoided.

A substantial meal should never be taken immediately before beginning gymnastics. A cup of coffee, tea or milk with a roll is harmless, and in some cases necessary, for elderly and delicate persons. After a hearty breakfast one or two hours should pass before beginning gymnastic exercises.

Persons desiring to obtain special knowledge of each apparatus are requested to consult Dr. ZANDER'S work, mentioned above. They will find there a detailed description of the application of each apparatus, as well as of the different movements of the muscles &c. &c.

III.

Organisation and sphere of activity of a Zander gymnastic Institute.

After having acquainted our readers with the object of the apparatus, we consider it necessary to give also a few details of the organisation of a Zander gymnastic Institute and to indicate briefly how gymnastics should be practised there.

• The apparatus are manufactured exclusively by the *»Göranssons Mekaniska Verkstad»* *Company Limited*, in Stockholm, under the control of Dr. ZANDER. Mr. ERNST GÖRANSSON C. E., director of this Company devotes himself with particular interest and an unusual degree of technical knowledge to the manufacture of these apparatus, the perfection and propagation of which are greatly due to his intelligence and energy. The following is what ZANDER himself says upon this subject in the preface to his book: »The spreading of my apparatus has indeed only become possible through the interest and work bestowed by Mr. GÖRANSSON on the technical and industrial development of my inventions. He has not only established in his Mechanical Works in Stockholm a special division for the thoroughly solid manufacture of the whole equipment of gymnastic and measuring apparatus, but he has also undertaken all the correspondence, has given, and will continue to give, all the advice and all the technical and economical information necessary for the establishment of Medico-Mechanical Zander Institutes abroad.»

On establishing a medical gymnastic Institute with the Zander apparatus, attention should first be paid to the premises. The house should be spacious, airy, and well ventilated; the gymnasium itself should have a floor-surface of 3,000 square feet. In addition there should be a consulting-room, sitting- and reading-room, a room for massage, a dressing-room, retiring- and ante-room.

Dr. G. SCHÜTZ, director of the Medico-Mechanical Zander Institute of Berlin, thus describes the reception of a patient at the Institute:

The new patient is submitted to a scrupulous examination and receives his prescription of movements as soon as the state of his health has been noted in the register of the patients. In this prescription are indicated, in a certain order, the apparatus which the patients have to use, and also the massage treatment, they may occasionally have to undergo. The patient passes from apparatus to apparatus, using them in the order prescribed. For this purpose he is directed by an instructor (medical assistant) who sees that the movement is made with suitable resistance and as often as it is prescribed. A number of young people, from 15 to 16 years of age, have the care of adjusting the apparatus according to the stature of the patient and the degree of resistance prescribed. During the exercise the patient

is instructed as to the correct way of breathing and he is made
to observe the proper interval of rest after each group of exercises. After some time the prescription is renewed with the
modifications that may be rendered necessary by the patient's
increased strength and greater flexibility of previously stiff
articulations &c. &c.

It would be particularly interesting to give here some statistics on the number of patients at the different Zander Institutes in Sweden and abroad. We have indeed at our disposal
solitary communications of the kind, found in papers and pam-
phlets, but to be able to pass an exact judgment we ought to
have complete, and authentic information of the number of patients at corresponding periods of the same years.

Therefore, since incomplete and inexact information might
occasion mistakes and various inconveniencies, we must limit our
statistics to the figures given by our Swedish gymnastic Institutes. Since 1887 these Institutes are by law bound to send in
regularly to medical authorities, reports of the number of patients and of the nature of diseases treated there. In his work
published in 1879 on the Zander Gymnastics and the Medico-
mechanical Institute in Stockholm, Dr. ZANDER has given in a
table the number of patients treated in the years 1865—78.

During the period of treatment in 1888—89 Dr. ZANDER's
Institute in Stockholm was frequented by 619, and in 1889—90
by 600 patients, forming the following pathological groups:

	Men.	Women.	Total.
Anæmia and Chlorosis	11	37	48
Obesity	12	6	18
Nervous diseases	111	47	158
Affections of the heart	165	59	224
» » » lungs	49	5	54
» » » digestive organs	155	29	184
» » » organs of locomotion . . .	169	57	226
Curvatures of the spine	14	119	133
Dietetic gymnastics	153	9	162
	839	368	1,207
Diseases not mentioned in the report	8	4	12
Total	847	372	1,219

During the above mentioned years, *The Medico-Mechanical Zander Gymnastic Institute at Östermalm* (North-Eastern part of Stockholm), of which I am the director, was in 1888—89 frequented by 325 patients, and in 1889 —90 by 331. If we add these figures to those of ZANDER the entire number of the persons who have used exclusively the *mechanical* Gymnastics of Stockholm[1] amounts to 934 in 1888—89 and to 931 in 1889—90.

With regard to the respective numbers of patients in the different Institutes, Dr. ZANDER'S is more frequented than the others.[2]

Reports from foreign Institutes on their frequentation and on the groups of diseases treated are found now and then in shorter publications. Amongst them we will mention the following: Report of Dr. HEILIGENTHAL in »Ärztliche Mittheilungen aus Baden», Annual XLII, 1888, page 33—39; in »Mittheilungen aus dem Grossherzoglichen Friedrichsbade», Karlsruhe 1889, page 3—16; ibid of Dr. H. NEBEL; ibid of Dr. G. SCHÜTZ »Der Kompass», p. 76; of Dr. HASEBROEK: »Über die Nervosität etc.», Hamburg 1891; »Mittheilungen aus dem Hamburger medico-mechan Institut vom 1890», Hamburg 1891, p. 57; of Dr. FRIEDMANN and of Dr. G. HEUCK: »Erster Jahresbericht des Medico-mechan. Zander Instituts in Mannheim», Mannheim 1889, p. 14; Dr. F. BÄHR, »Prospekt N:o 2 etc. Med. Mech. Institut in Karlsruhe 1891».

These patients, of an age between 4 and 80 years, were either representatives of all the diseases treated previously by medical Gymnastics, or persons, who, without any special ailments, used gymnastics because of their generally strengthening effects, and as a preservative (dietetic gymnastics) against the consequences of a sedentary life, or work requiring one-sided exertion of certain muscles; or, finally, schoolboys, considered of *too weak* a constitution to support the ordinary pedagogic

---

[1] *The gymnastic Institute of Södermalm* (Southern part of Stockholm) possesses only a comparatively small number of apparatus, and the patients are treated by manual as well as by mechanical Gymnastics.

[2] In the same years also the Royal Central Gymnastic Institute had in 1888—89, 542 patients to 468 in 1889—90. As to the Orthopedic Institute, it counted in 88—89, 547 patients and in 89—90, 569. These two establishments have Government-allowances and are therefore bound to have a great number of free places which are counted in the figures above.

gymnastics, and who were consequently sent to these gymnastics as being the most perfect, and, as developing-gymnastics, best answering pedagogic purposes. (ZANDER ibid p. 16).

IV.

Vibration in the medico-mechanical Zander gymnastic treatment.

Before passing to a special examination of the different groups of diseases and describing the importance of gymnastics for the preservation of health and the development of the body, we will point out an important feature in the treatment, which, properly speaking, belongs to the description of the apparatus. borrowing from a work called »Die Erschütterungen in der Zander'schen Heilgymnastik» published by Dr. KARL HASE-BROEK of Hamburg, the description of a kind of movement that we may consider as a *specialty* of our gymnastic method. »When ZANDER», says that author, »introduced mechanical apparatus in gymnastics, for measured application of the movements and to extend to wider circles the benefit of medical gymnastics, he gave special attention to vibratory and percutient operations. After many years' work and exertion he has now perfected apparatus that work with a remarkable precision, adapting themselves to the various requirements of the patients. It is scarcely needful to say that these apparatus for vibration are particulary entitled to be considered a specialty of the Zander gymnastics. No gymnast is able to give these purely mechanical movements so well, so regularly, and for the same length of time. NEUMANN, an ancient writer on this subject, mentioning the beneficial effects of vibrations, says that it is difficult to apply them when a larger number of patients have to be treated, and that they require *such a degree of dexterity* and *such development of strength* on the part of the gymnast, that even if the successful effects were greater still, it would scarcely be possible to recommend them. It is indeed the great

merit of ZANDER to have turned to profit the power of mechanical apparatus for these various purposes. The apparatus producing the vibrations and percussions answer the most varied
requirements, and the patient himself can modify the effect of
the apparatus by simple manipulations, sometimes merely by a
more or less strong pressure.

HARTELIUS,[1] also writes as follows: »As regards the vibrations, it is necessary to notice that they must be given *vigorously*
and with perseverance in order to be effective. The exercise is
tiring and therefore machines have long been employed.»

These vibrations which can be applied to all the parts of the
body, principally appear in the following forms:

Foot-vibration.

Perineal vibration.

Shoulder- and shoulder-blade-vibration.

Back-vibration.

Vibration of the lumbar region.

Sacrum-vibration.

Hip-vibration.

Chest-vibration.

Epigastrium-vibration.

Vibration of the transverse colon, of the small intestine, of
the cæcum and of the descending colon.

Lateral vibration of the knee and bend of the knee.

Vibration of the hip-nerves.

Neck-vibration (occipital).

Forehead-vibration.

Temple-, ear-, nose-, neck-vibration.

Throat-vibration.

Vibrations running along the arms, thighs, knees and calves.

Arm-, forearm- and hand-vibration.

The influence of these vibrations on different parts of the
body has not yet been studied in its minutest details and consequently is not perfectly known at the present moment.

On the general influence, however, experience has taught
us a great many indications that ZANDER has summed up in
the following rules:

---

[1] T. I. HARTELIUS. Lehrbuch der schwedischen Heilgymnastik. Leipzig 1860, p. 98.

A vibrating object, brought into contact with the soft tissues of the body, exercises on these an effect of rapidly alternating expansion and pressure. This accelerates the circulation in the capillaries and lymph-vessels, increases the reabsorption and causes the morbid infiltration of the tissues to disappear.[1]

Of a still greater importance, and particularly instructive, is the observation of the influence of the vibration on the heart and circulation, which phenomena Dr. HASEBROEK has principally made the object of interesting researches.

He thus sums up the effect of these vibrations:

I. Diminution of the frequency of the pulse.
II. Vasomotory increase of the tension of the arteries.
III. Raising of the tone of the heart-muscles.
IV. Increase of blood-pressure.

We will further point out here a circumstance which nobody has hitherto mentioned, and which constitutes a powerful additional proof, in favour of gymnastic treatment in heart-diseases. At the time when the writer of this was Dr. ZANDER's medical assistant, as well as since in the course of our own practice, we remember a large number of patients suffering from heart-disease who have all died a sudden, if not instantaneous death by paralysis of the heart, but never has such a case occurred to any one under gymnastic treatment. Nor do there occur instances of deaths of the kind either at the Royal Central or at the Orthopedic Institute. Such events could scarcely have been kept secret at a time when gymnastics and medicine were in fierce conflict with one another, for, what a deadly weapon would it not have been against gymnastics, in the hands of the adversary, to be able to relate such an accident.

This has not occurred, however, and for our part we are fully convinced that this fact is not due exclusively to hazard, but finds its explanation in the circumstance that the heart is slightly stimulated by the gymnastic movement and the methodical respiration. This argument cannot, it is true, weigh heavily in the balance of scientific proofs, but it is worth attention as a mere fact, and, as such, deserves to be stated.

[1] ZANDER ibid. p. 84.

The knowledge of the effect of vibrations on the heart has been enlarged by the researches of Dr. HASEBROEK and we cannot too warmly recommend these researches to the study of our colleagues. He also mentions numerous results of experiments with respect to the influence of vibration on the breathing (on the secretion of carbonic acid) and referring to these results, he expresses the hope that these facts, obtained by means of experiments, may contribute to the final solution of many still unsolved questions. We support the following conclusions of the author, at the end of his work: »Vibrations, combined with other gymnastic exercises, without which they would be too one-sided and of too passing an effect, are of the most remarkable use and have the very best results. They facilitate the circulation of the blood in the peripheral veins and ameliorate the nutrition of the muscles in stimulating the heart to greater activity, and in promoting the compensatory hypertrophy of the heart, so salutary in these cases. Here the vibrations constitute an indispensable auxiliary of the inappreciable gymnastic remedies.»

He continues these reflections by expressing his admiration for the invaluable inventions of Dr. ZANDER and regretting that medical science has not everywhere, as in Sweden, employed medical gymnastics for heart-diseases.

Quoting the well known words of Professor MURRAY: »It is to be regretted that this method of treating heart-diseases has scarcely passed beyond the frontiers of our country», he concludes by saying that fortunately these words are no longer true of Germany, thanks to the extraordinary and highly meritorious efforts of HEILIGENTHAL and NEBEL.[1] »Still we cannot but regret that such a number of physicians continue to show themselves indifferent to the Zander method and to medical gymnastics in general. In the conflict[2] which is still going on between the *manual* and the *med. mechanical* methods of

---

[1] Dr. SCHÜTZ of Berlin and other esteemed colleagues have also been working with great energy and real success to make our method appreciated in Germany, and indefatigably continue their work for this end.

[2] We cannot say that such a conflict actually exists in Sweden, for it belongs to the past.

gymnastics, both methods are often abandoned — the handle
is thrown after the axe — to the great damage of gymnastics.»

_____

V.

Dietetic Gymnastics on the Zander method.

The public has gradually come to recognise that gymnastic treatment is beneficial to a great number of diseases, and,
just as there have been great difficulties for medical gymnastics
in winning a right to existence, so a healthy man only slowly
perceives the fact that gymnastics are necessary for maintain-
ing his general health and his vital strength. This vitality
which finds an expression in the energy with which the organism reacts against external pernicious influences, makes man
independent of the manifold inward and outward influences which
limit his mental and physical activity; it even enables him to
undergo tests to which a less vigorous person would succumb.
The same vitality appears in the perfection with which all the
organs work together to ward off dangers threatening the whole
organism, if one organ be overstrained or weakened. Long or
repeated illnesses always diminish this beneficial reaction and
make the cure more difficult.

»The stimulating and strengthening effect that systematical
exercises possess in a very high degree, are consequently of vast
importance in the treatment of chronic diseases and in con-
valescence. It is not only illnesses, however, that undermine
vital strength; unreasonable habits of life, want of light, air
and exercise, principally while overstraining our intellectual
powers: all that concurs to wear out the vital strength, makes
young people prematurely old, and makes an originally healthy
and vigorous body a field for all sorts of debilities and infir-
mities. Now the mission of dietetic gymnastics is to prevent
this evil by means of exercise, as soon as it is a case of want
of exercise or insufficient and one-sided activity, as with the great

majority of the inhabitants of towns in consequence of their oc‧
cupations. For these persons dietetic gymnastics are an abso‧
lute necessity, as anyone who knows the least about the necess‧
ity of exercising one's muscles, will easily understand. [1]

›There are indeed very few men whose professions require
a variety of movements and daily muscle-exercises. Their num‧
ber is infinitely small in comparison to the multitude who, all
their life, lack systematical exercises, while these are absolutely
necessary for the maintenance of health and capacity to work.
The assertion that gymnastics are superfluous, because one is
enjoying good health, is as senseless as it would be to set out
on a journey through a desert without provisions, for the rea‧
son that one does not feel any hunger at starting. As a rule
we do not mind other needs than such as punish us immediately
for our neglect by pain or suffering, or such as give satisfac‧
tion or enjoyment. Regular and complex bodily exercise is a
necessity the satisfying of which rewards us by a sensation of
well-being, by enjoyment of life and by increase of mental and
physical strength. The neglect of this requirement causes in us,
a feeling of weakness and weariness, depression, and a series
of ailments and sufferings which infuse bitterness into our lives,
weaken our energy and in manifold ways limit our capacity for
work and enjoyment. The need of exercise does not indeed
present itself with the same urgency and imperiousness as many
others, or, in other words, a man enjoying good health may neg‧
lect exercise some time, before the inconvenience makes itself
felt. This circumstance offers a welcome pretext for indifference
and love of ease; — not feeling ill, why this unnecessary trouble?
Thus the vital energy is ever decreasing, though the body have
an appearance of endurance, and of being in excellent health.
We say appearance, for we, men, need an energetic, exercised
vigorous body which can carry out the impulses of the will, a
body with a tenacity to resist successfully all the sufferings and
disagreeables of life.›

Considering all this world of officials, merchants, teachers
and men of learning who lead a sedentary life, who are chiefly
engaged in mental work, who neither will nor can satisfy the
want of complex bodily exercise, we cannot understand this in-

[1] ZANDER ibid. p. 19.

difference, all the more as we know that this excessive mental
work is frequently combined with a sensual, effeminate mode
of life. The following is what happens in most cases: they work
till a late hour and get up late in the morning; then follow
six or seven hours' hard work at the office or bureau in small
and badly ventilated rooms. In the winter-season there are further dinner- and supper-parties, card-parties, with obligatory cigar-
smoke &c. How much time will there be left for rest and necessary sleep? In the long run the healthiest organism cannot support this, and ill-used nature generally takes full revenge.
As soon as evil results appear, they try to make compensation
for mistakes committed, by giving half an hour morning and
evening to »a constitutional». Walking, riding and driving are
to a certain degree gymnastic exercises, but they are not systematical. One can determine the degree of the effort, but not that
of the strength the body must develop, nor the power exercised
on the body. In walking, for instance, the vigour of the movement does not only depend on the length of time, the speed,
the character of the ground, but also on the weight of the body,
which has to be supported by the legs. And it is by no means
certain that the strength of the leg-muscles is in proportion
to the weight of the body. A number of such incalculable
factors assert their influence also in equitation and driving.

These various kinds of exercise are indeed infinitely better
than none at all, but their value is often exaggerated. In walking
a few muscles only are in activity and that even incompletely,
as the muscles of the legs are almost the only muscles needed
to set the body in motion and keep it upright. Good exercise
requires above all a sufficient alternation between work and
rest; but there is no attention paid to this requirement in walking, especially as regards the back-muscles which are subjected
to a continual tension. That is the reason why weak persons
feel a pain in their backs after a walk of some length. Then,
the muscles ought to have occasion to contract and to relax
completely, which neither takes place in walking nor in the
other movements of daily life. Out-of-door exercise is nevertheless of great value, because then the respiration is complete.

Sport having of late become the fashion, we must examine
also more closely its value and influence. Fencing-clubs, riding-

schools, free gymnastics, cycling and skating have their warm
partisans, their enthusiastic admirers, sometimes turned into real
fanatics. We will not by any means dissuade them from these
excellent exercises which are of great value for the preservation
of health. May the friends of sport make proselytes in ever increasing numbers! But — we must remember that a great number
of perfectly healthy people are not adapted for sport with its useful
and agreeable exercises; and besides, many of the movements
occurring are exclusive enough and develop only certain muscles, —
not at the expense of the others but certainly without satisfying the
wants of the latter. These exercises cannot in any way measure
themselves with the complex forms of medical gymnastic treatment.

Free gymnastics, or at least the Swedish pedagogic method
of Ling, are most akin to our treatment. By the multiplicity of
positions and corresponding movements, free gymnastics strive
to attain the general development of the organism. It is easily
understood, however, that these movements cannot be indivi-
dualised to the same degree as by medical gymnastics. As we
have said already, the act of overcoming a gradually increasing
resistance produced by means of the hand or of some artificial
apparatus, is our idea and the secret of our art. The resistance
overcome by the gymnast is represented by the weight of the
body, but his weight presents a great difference in different persons. As for instance in the case of two men making a spring,
one of them weighing e. g. 16 st. the other 8 st., when the
leg-muscles of the one have to lift up a weight twice as great
as the other, though they may be very much weaker. It may
be even that the first is overstrained, while the second may
not have had enough work for his muscles. We will not follow
this example into details, for we have not the least wish to en-
tice away a single adept of sport. We, medical gymnasts, have
indeed sufficient work with the ages which do not exactly go in
for sport: from about 50 years of age, the limbs gradually become
stiff and no longer adapt themselves to the requirements of sport.
It is then that our careful, complex gymnastic movements will no
doubt be welcome. There certainly exist persons who have trained
their bodies for sport, and nothing will hinder them from continuing as long as their strength will allow it. Sooner or later, however, the time will come when the weight of years will

make itself felt, and, as the necessity for exercise will continue, such persons will find compensation by trusting themselves to our medical gymnastics.

The following objection to gymnastics as a dietetic means is also sometimes heard: »What are they good for, these artificial remedies, which our ancestors knew nothing about, nor ever used? It is easy to answer this question and we will do so in order to leave no pretext to indifference and love of ease.

Our times are entirely different from those of our ancestors with their warlike exploits and simple habits. Then, the exercise of arms formed an essential part of education, life had nothing of the refined and enervating habits of the 19th century, the struggle for existence was neither so severe, nor so wearying as in our days — the ardour of speculation was still in its infancy, nobody expected to get rich in a trice, for fortune was frequently attained by industry, manual *dexterity* and economy.

Which of us for instance would actually be inclined to cut and saw for himself the provision of wood requisite to warm his house and to be his own gardener? Such useful exercise then belonged to the daily occupations of our Scandinavian forefathers as to those of other nations.

Let us now examine how it is with womankind from the point of view of dietetic gymnastics. Here no doubt matters are still worse. The exercise of women is so entirely one-sided that it is there we find the cause of the nervous complaints from which the women of our times suffer to such a degree. They comfort themselves by saying that both at home and abroad they have so much exercise, so many hours are devoted to walking, visiting, and to the exercise of dancing, which indeed fills half and even whole nights. We need not explain the value of such exercise. Every body will acknowledge that the exercise of the muscles must be particularly important for woman in whose entire being the activity of the nervous system plays the principal part.

Free exercises are indeed introduced in our Swedish Young Ladies' Schools, but the opportunity ceases with the sixteenth or seventeenth year, and what is then done to strengthen and confirm health? All systematical work generally seems tiresome to women, who therefore in gymnastics see a real torture that they had much rather avoid. Now, as the nerves of women are much more excitable than those of men, nervous diseases find good soil in woman-kind. There is only one way of preventing and struggling against these sufferings and that is to strengthen the nervous system by the development of the muscles and the induration of the body.

Bathing is also very useful and should be combined with gymnastics. It will be the duty of the physician therefore, to insist on the necessity and usefulness of gymnastics, for very few ladies indeed attend our gymnastics of their *own* accord. By gymnastic exercises of some months they easily conquer the weariness which is usually felt in the beginning. This weariness does not imply overstraining of the muscles, but as we have said above, it is a symptom of a nervous disease. It is true that in old times a woman's work in the house offered greater variety and brought on greater bodily fatigue than now-a-days; besides, women were formerly more vigorous and their offspring consequently was stronger and had greater power of endurance. The loss of an hour a day, so highly estimated when it is devoted to gymnastics, beneficial though they be to body and mind, could easily be compensated by putting aside a number of useless occupations.

We cannot resist the wish to quote on this subject an authority like ZANDER: ›Woman does not need strong muscles; the nervous system and the organs of vegetative functions are predominant in her. But as muscular exercises are *effective means, impossible to substitute*, for keeping the nerves and other organs in a healthy and vigorous state, they are equally necessary to man and woman. They are even of particular importance to woman as a preservative against various abdominal and uterine disorders.»

48

VI.

Developing-Gymnastics on the Zander method.

In Sweden, which rightfully may be called »the promised land» of pedagogic gymnastics, it is sometimes a subject of grave inquiry, whether school-gymnastics or medical gymnastics are to be preferred for certain children. The following is what ZANDER says in one of his papers: »The mental strain, so contrary to nature and so exclusive, which is now required from children, must incontestably overexcite the nervous system and sow the seeds of the malady, characteristic of our times, — neurasthenia. The nervous system is weakened by the intellectual over-exertion, the muscles by want of bodily exercise, and thus the development of the body is arrested. Boys become weak, sickly and nervous; this is also the case with young girls, even in a higher degree, and scoliosis often accompanies this weakness. Any one expert in these matters will acknowledge that in a similar, more or less abnormal state, the principal mission of gymnastics is not to give the child the agility attained in ordinary school-gymnastics by springing, climbing, arm-movements &c. &c., but the thing is rather to strenghten the system by cautious, progressive exercises, comprising the whole muscular system, to reestablish the lost equilibrium of the organism, to turn the development into its natural course, and thus to avoid the over-excitement of the nervous system. Medical gymnastics alone can effect this. If they succeed in promoting this end, if the vital strength is raised, and the economy of the entire body displays abundance instead of the want that was reigning before, — then may ordinary school-gymnastics be employed to give to the children as much agility and power over their body as is possible and useful.»

We only understand the justness of these, perhaps somewhat strong expressions, if we pay attention to the circumstance that, with us, school-gymnastics are obligatory in all boys' schools, and now also in many girls' schools, and that pupils cannot be excused from them, unless they present a certificate from the school- or family-physician. But — physicians are of different opinions as to the maladies that may be considered sufficient reason for excuse: one will declare school-gymnastics unsuitable for such and such a child, while another will say just the contrary. For the purpose of obtaining unanimity on this point, in 1887 I set the Association of Swedish Gymnasts the following question as a subject of discussion: »Which are the maladies requiring abstention from school-gymnastics and what proceeding is to be adopted with regard to the children in such cases?» A committee composed of three school- and three medical-gymnasts was elected which submitted its reports to the general discussion of the 10th of December in the same year. It was agreed on the necessity of dispensation for children affected with the following diseases: ear-diseases, accompanied by giddiness and vomiting; chorea, epilepsy; organic defects of the heart; palpitation of the heart (tachycardia): chronic affections of the lungs; bronchitis (especially when affected by the inevitable dust of the gymnasium); perityphlitis or appendicitis; albuminuria; coxalgia; gibbousness.[1] For the majority of these diseases medical gymnastic treatment was judged the best substitute for school-gymnastic exercises. Still it would be only on the authority of a certificate that a pupil going through a course of medical gymnastics would be dispensed from school-gymnastics. That is what was stated on the paper; but in reality there remains now as before a large portion of children who, declared unfit for school-gymnastics, get no gymnastic treatment at all. In the same discussion there was, from many sides, insisted on the necessity of organising in the schools, a so called sick-section with special, suitable gymnastic treatment. A great many children of poor parents would thus be enabled to attend developing-gymnastics at the expense of the state, and that would be all the more desirable that country towns do not generally possess medical gymnastic Institutes. The establishment of a similar section, however, re-

---

[1] For scoliosis preference was given to medical gymnastics; but as an opportunity of such treatment is not everywhere to be found, it has not been enumerated among those counted as a cause of abstention from school-gymnastics.

4

quires a greater number of gymnasts, a more generous remuneration to gymnastic professors, and hitherto we have remained in *statu quo* on these two points. When the parents of weak or sick children are in easy circumstances, we do not hesitate to encourage them to confide their children to a medical gymnastic Institute, if there be one within their reach. It is probable that in other countries it happens as with us, that children dispensed for some reason or other from ordinary school-gymnastics, do not receive any treatment at all, at the time of life most favorable for the development of the body. During several years we have given gymnastics gratuitously at our Institute to poor children of both sexes from National Schools, always requesting the school-physician to send by preference the weakest children, and the results obtained have always been most satisfactory. Dr. ZANDER has also in the course of time gathered rich experience in this direction.

In fact many parents might let their children profit by medical gymnastic treatment, but they do not, from *indifference* or other reasons, and it is also a fact that we, gymnasts, need the firm support of our colleagues for the realisation of our ideas. Medical science would gain much if our efforts were supported by their energetic collaboration. Now people think they do quite enough by sending their young folks a few weeks in summer to the seaside, up to the mountains or into some country place, and though we are not in any way opposed to such proceedings, yet we must insist on the fact that this short time of recreation, however beneficial it may be, cannot be compared with the results of several months' gymnastic treatment at our Institutes. We even declare that often the holiday expenses greatly exceed those of gymnastic treatment during the whole winter.

VII.

The use of medico-mechanical Zander Gymnastics for morbid affections.

In the following pages we will consider gymnastics as a *curative means* of acknowledged value, or, at least, as an effective auxiliary in the removal or relief of a great number of morbid phenomena. Before passing to the more or less brief examination of various diseases and to the result of their treatment, we take the liberty of quoting, by way of introduction, the opinion of a German physician, which gives evidence of profound and special knowledge:[1] »We have continually had to deal with chronic states and diseases, and in our curative exercises we take care not to struggle against them by extraordinary, violent means, destroying directly the morbid changes or the agents of the malady. On the contrary we exert ourselves to do so only by strengthening and stimulating the power given to the organism itself to remove abnormal states, in a word, we work in the manner of a dietetic cure. A considerable time, amounting to months, is generally wanted for that kind of cure.

»As regards the curative plan in general, we must insist above all on a certain duration of treatment, for we have in most cases to do with chronic diseases and sickly dispositions. By sickly dispositions we understand the tendency of the organism to fall into certain morbid states, such as excessive obesity, nervous over-excitement &c. &c.

As a rule this disposition is of some duration, even when the abnormal symptoms themselves have disappeared. It would be unreasonable to demand immediate and lasting success by one single course of gymnastic treatment. It is evident that these patients ought rather to continue the treatment, destined to contend with their predispositions, long after they believe themselves cured. When individuals obtain greater power of

---

[1] Erster Jahresbericht über die Wirksamkeit des Gymn. Orthopäd. Instituts in Mannheim 1889 von FRIEDMANN & HEUCK, p. 11—14.

resistance, medical gymnastics may certainly be substituted by other, and more simple forms of exercise: equitation, ordinary gymnastics, some kind of sport &c. But, with suitable intervals, when the question is improvement of health, they ought to come back for some months at a time to the treatment of the Institute. Unfortunately these facts are neither sufficiently known and appreciated by the public, nor by part of the medical body. It has happened to us that a patient with an almost continual head-ache (hemicrania) during a period of 12 years, and due to excessive anæmia (a disease, which as we know, is exceedingly obstinate) expected remarkable improvement after a fortnight, whereas whole months are required to show appreciable effects. Another expected, after a month, the disappearance of an obstinate constipation which had lasted for years.

»As a rule, *two months* must be counted as the minimum of time to be thought of for the attainment of a sufficiently effective result; other cases will require infinitely more time, and it is necessary that there should be a clear understanding on this matter both by the patient and the family-doctor. The view of the extent of attainable results can thus immediately be brought to a just measure. Too little value must not be given to them. There are circumstances of indisputable im· portance, where Swedish medical gymnastics are more effective than any other treatment, and as instances I will mention *fatty degeneration of the heart* and the early stages of curvatures of the spine. In all these circumstances the results are frequently most thorough: subjectively for the sensation of the patient, objectively for the physician who examines. In other cases where the treatment is generally considered suitable, the effects are obvious, often even *brilliant*, considering the gentle and careful proceeding of the method. Certain symptoms of gastric disorders of nervous origin, of vertigo, of cases of hyperæmia have disappeared rapidly enough, without doing so in the almost instantaneous manner with which a dose of calomel for instance, dispels cardiac hydropsy. But, as we have said, the character of most affections submitted to our treatment is generally such that they cannot, by the means actually at our disposal, be dispelled as by a magic wand. On the authority of patients who have felt relieved from all their ailments, and, so to speak, born to a new life, we might often have wished to claim the honour of having effected perfect cures; but it was evident that we had not before us a definite cure, that sooner or later *relapses* would occur, and, as a matter of fact, that has frequently happened.

»As we have said, however, the gymnastic treatment does not give, in this respect, results inferior to those of any other method of treatment under the same conditions.

»We have briefly indicated above the morbid states in which gymnastic treatment is able to offer special advantages and opportunities: first, abnormal states of the locomotion-apparatus; then functional diseases of the nervous system; those of the circulation and the heart; disorders of nutrition and assimilation, and finally the atony of the intestines, i. e. constipation. In other domains of morbid disorders, gymnastics will only exceptionally take the first rank amongst curative agents, even if the improved assimilation and the exercise of the muscles be beneficial, as happens in almost every case of chronic disease which displays itself in decreased strength.»

We must therefore, emphasise the fact that in our curative method nobody should expect a particularly rapid change in the morbid state. Unfortunately it is exactly on this point that our patients indulge in illusions which may be dangerous enough for their future, considering that the success of a medical gymnastic cure is always in proportion to the length of time given to it.

May we also be permitted to insist a little more strongly on the fact that a considerable number of physicians refuse to recognise the importance of medical gymnastics, and, therefore, frequently declare useless and superfluous the expense occasioned by this kind of treatment. But the public of our days insists on knowing what we, physicians, mean to do for the well-being of our patients, and it has fortunately more taste and susceptibility for hygienic means such as air, baths, gymnastic treatment, than for drugs. The number of our patients is also reinforced especially by persons who instinctively turn to their physician with a request to let them try gymnastic treatment. They are comparatively few, to whom the physician gives advice of *this* kind from his own initiative.

According to our plan we will now successively review the
different groups of maladies which ordinarily come under our
treatment, only examining in detail ›gymnastic diseases› i. e.
those for which medical gymnastics may more or less be considered a specific.

a. Diseases of the heart.

To ›the gymnastic diseases› belong in the first place the
morbid affections of the heart and vascular system, and it is
exactly on this point we have to struggle against the greatest
prejudices in medical circles. The assertion that for these affections, gymnastic exercises may be put on a level with digitalis,
strophantus and other known cardiac remedies, seems incom-
prehensible to them. They consider our mode of treatment due
to erroneous judgment and believe that we hold out to our patients hopes, or certainties, of improvement which it will be
impossible to realise. This is how the matter stands in reality:
it is not here a question of attempting to cure organic diseases of
the heart; but still it is possible to us to soothe or remove by
systematical gymnastic treatment a considerable part of the
painful symptoms, such as the continual *dyspnœa*, œdema, palpitations, anxiety, and in fact, we are able to delay the deadly
issue for years. Dr NEBEL shares this view: ›In Sweden›, says
he, ›the fact that disorders of the circulation as principal cause of
pathological symptoms in the affections of the heart, can, as far
as they arise from mechanical causes, be cured by mechanical
means — this fact, first recognised and proclaimed not by medical men, but by the renowned P. H. LING and his pupils, at
the beginning of this century led to a most successful treatment
of the above affections. On learning that, for thirty years,
gymnastic treatment has always and increasingly been used and
recommended even by the physicians of Scandinavia [1] as being
rational and confirmed by practice; that persons, suffering from
affections of the heart, form a considerable portion of our
patients, and that eminent Swedish physicians (H. SÄTHER-
BERG, G. ZANDER, V. VRETLIND, T. HARTELIUS, R. MURRAY &c.)

---

[1] By the name of ›Scandinavia›, the author undoubtedly means Sweden
alone, considering that with our neighbours, Norway and Denmark, gymnastic treatment has not by far made equal progress.

have written on the subject, there is every reason to, be aston-
ished that this curative method has not, until quite a recent
period, been mentioned by our writers with regard to the treatment of cardiac affections, and that it can have remained absolutely unknown to the mass of the medical body. After Dr.
HEILIGENTHAL, Professor LEYDEN was the first German writer
who to a certain extent did justice to the merits of the Swedes,
regarding the mechanical treatment of disorders in the circulation.»

Dr. ZANDER indicates still more precisely the importance of
gymnastic movement for affections of the heart, which induces
us to quote with pleasure his own words: [1] »In cardiac affections
the object of gymnastics is to facilitate the action of this organ
and to increase or diminish its contractile power. To attain
this end, slight contractions of the voluntary muscles are used
first. By the work of the muscles, occasioned by relatively
slight active movements which must only gradually be increased,
the functional irritation causes a flow of blood to the organs
in activity, while the mechanical effect of the contraction must
accelerate the circulation in the capillaries and veins. Consequently the pressure of the blood diminishes in the large
arteries and this naturally lessens the resistance that the heart
is called upon to overcome. The result is a soothing influence
on the heart, which can empty itself completely, even in the
case that its contractile power should be very slight.

»If the contractions of the heart are *imperfect*, they become
more perfect, owing to the diminution of blood-pressure, and it
is natural that this should have a beneficial influence on the
circulation and nutrition of this organ. A gradual improvement and strengthening of the cardiac muscles are thus obtained,
being exactly the desiderata in many pathological phenomena
of the heart, as, for instance, fatty degeneration. Under such
circumstances, the slight increase in the action of the heart,
resulting from carefully made active movements, cannot but be
advantageous. The effect of active movements, to accelerate
the circulation, will naturally increase in the same proportion
as these movements are complex and varied, or, in other words,
as a wider range of circulation is submitted to their influence.
This theory, therefore, is not in harmony with the seemingly

[1] Nord. med. Ark. Vol. IV p. 11.

current opinion, that, for affections of the heart, gymnastic treatment should be limited to leg-movements only. It may be added that the peripheric circulation of the blood is promoted, and the action of the heart facilitated by passive mechanical operations such as rubbings and kneadings, which produce contractions and repeated evacuations of blood in the capillaries and peripheric veins; or by vibrations [1] bringing on the contraction and emptying of the small arteries, as these movements have precisely for object the increase of the work which the elasticity of the arteries must effect; finally also by movements promoting a deeper and more perfect respiration.›

. Those are briefly the fundamental laws on which our theories are based, and which are ever more developed by explorers in this domain. Gymnastics produce a more equal distribution of the blood by diminishing the surplus in the veins and conveying it into the arterial vessels, without, however, simultaneously increasing the blood-pressure. The contractions of the heart are facilitated through the lessening of pressure in the system of aorta, which is also attained by the acceleration of the peripheric circulation by means of passive movements and mechanical operations. Active movements dilate the muscular vessels by reflex action. The heart-muscles are strengthened, and their nutrition ameliorated, which is manifested by the diminution of a previous dilatation, and by the production of a compensatory hypertrophy. Therefore the essence of the treatment of heart-diseases, according to Dr. ZANDER, consists of the three following cardinal points:

1. *The acceleration of the peripheric circulation* effected by the purely mechanical influences of gymnastics on veins and capillaries.

2. *The facilitation of the action of the heart*, resulting from the diminution of blood-pressure in the arterial system, either by the dilatation of the arteries by reflex action, or by greater consumption of blood in the muscles employed. In this way the heart has less resistance to overcome and can therefore more completely contract and empty itself in the aorta. This diminution of resistance exercises on the heart a soothing in-

---

[1] See our chapter on ›Vibration.›

fluence, though it must contract more rapidly, so that the arterial pressure may not be below that necessary for the maintenance of the circulation.

3. *The acceleration of the pulmonic circulation* by the deeper and stronger respiration that should always accompany gymnastic exercise, an auxiliary which not only stimulates both the pulmonic and the systemic circulation, but produces an essential improvement in the whole constitution of the patient.

We ought also to say a few words of a curative method, which in Germany, to a certain degree presents itself as a rival of our Swedish method of treatment. This method is the *Terrainkur* or »mountain-climbing» of Dr. OERTEL. As this learned physician maintains that his cure constitutes a general remedy and not a special one for disorders in the circulation, a mechanical dietetic proceeding which is not in any way in opposition to the use of our remedies, we claim with NEBEL all these advantages for our own method of treatment. »The Swedish method or ZANDER's method, says NEBEL (p. 196) is undoubtedly gentler, more easily put into practice and less expensive, and besides, infinitely more advisable for invalids than the ascent of mountains.» OERTEL's method cannot exercise a soothing effect on the action af the heart, it is too powerful a stimulant, and therein lies a great danger to a great many persons affected with heart-diseases. We, Swedish gymnasts, know by experience that physicians do not trust their cardiopathic patients to us without scruples and a certain anxiety, and consequently we have never been able to understand how that dangerous »Terrainkur» can have been so generally adopted. It is true that the danger is not so great when OERTEL's cure is directed and superintented by a careful physician who has studied the nature of the evil in every particular case. Unfortunately this method has become fashionable and is practised by everybody without necessary reflection and control, and »last but not least», generally also without the least precaution. We perfectly recognise OERTEL's merit, in so far as he has taught us to contend against hydremic states by the »dry cure», but we have nevertheless our scruples with respect to his »mountain-cure.» ZANDER says with regard to this: »The ascent of mountains may become, I think, a useful complementary treatment, when medical

58

gymnastics have effected in the patient so great an improvement
that he can be exposed to the violent fatigues of this kind
of sport.» Dr. HEILIGENTHAL, sharing ZANDER'S opinion, says
on the same subject: [1] The controversies among the partisans of the various methods of mechanical treatment of affections of the heart are not yet suppressed. The partisans
of manual gymnastics and those of ZANDER'S gymnastics extol
their respective methods, and the initiate in OERTEL's method
do likewise. The truth is no doubt to be found between the
extremes, [2] each method has its advantages and successful results.
A judicious individualisation will attribute to each of the methods its proper merits, since the well-timed combination
of both modes of treatment will be necessary for obtaining
good results. However, any one who has opportunity for treating affections of the heart both after the medical gymnastic
Zander method and OERTEL's method (and we, HEILIGENTHAL,
are frequently in a position to apply these two methods, sepa-
rately or combined) will decidedly give preference to the Zander
method, the indications of which are more extensive than those
of OERTEL's method. The patients who are no longer permitted
to use OERTEL's cures, may still frequently, with advantage and
without fear, use ZANDER's apparatus. *It even often happens* that
ZANDER'S method enables them to attempt again the indisputable
pleasures of the mountain-cure. While ZANDER's method is
blamed for its length of treatment, there is also every reason to
recognise the advantage of less danger. ZANDER's mechanical
gymnastics can be used at any time, while, for the mountain-

---

[1] Mittheilungen aus dem Grossherzogl. Friedrichsbade in Baden-Baden.
Karlsruhe 1889 p. 9.

[2] We cannot help mentioning with respect to this, Dr. ZANDER's expressions, when we were discussing this opinion. ›This view of the matter›,
he said ›seems strange. One of the methods (gymnastics) can be used in
all cases and has manifested itself *free from all danger;* the other (OERTEL's
cure) is absolutely impossible in *many* cases, and has more than once
shown itself *dangerous;* therefore I question how one can say, with HEILI-
GENTHAL, that the truth, regarding the superiority of the two methods,
would not be found on either side, but in a middle course, that is, in a
method that would certainly be less dangerous than the latter, but also
less practicable than the former.›

cure, a suitable [1] season must be awaited, if, owing to the circumstances, it is necessary to undertake long, fatiguing and
expensive journeys to »sanatoriums» in mountainous countries.
The medical gymnastic Institute of Friedrichsbad sometimes
receives patients suffering from diseases of the heart who are
unable to walk the distance from their dwelling to the Institute,
and it would indeed be perilous to prescribe mountain-climbing
to such patients. After a few weeks only of medical gymnastics, these patients frequently surprise us by the news that
without effort and difficulty, they have been able to take a
walk on the neighbouring heights.»

OERTEL's method has further been of great use by drawing
the attention of the medical world to our Swedish medical gymnastics, and has thus led them to recognise that our gymnastic
treatment is under all circumstances the most suitable. It would
seem as if physicians, and especially patients, ought to understand at last that they have in medical gymnastics their surest
support and their greatest comfort.

Another mode of treatment in these diseases of the heart,
is, at least with us, generally liked and frequently used, namely the summer-cure of Nauheim, or in other words, salt
baths with the addition of a large percentage of carbonic acid.
All our Swedish bathing-places at the present moment use artificial baths. In my quality of physician at a bathing establishment, I have tried these baths several years, and I appreciate
them highly as auxiliaries, but always use them simultaneously
with gymnastic treatment. A special variety of gymnastic treatment has also been used at Nauheim by the late Dr. SCHOTT,
but, according to reports of Swedish physicians, it is most primitive and imperfect.

Foreign bathing-places which, in summer, are frequented
by thousands of invalids, should for their use organise regular
gymnastic Institutes, and we are fully convinced that the results
obtained would amply repay the expense that the founding of
these Institutes would entail. We, physicians at Swedish Baths,
with our favorable experience of several decades, have only good

---

[1] To remedy this inconvenience, they have constructed in Germany a
kind of apparatus for ascending mountains, a »curiosity» on the description of which it would be useless to lose time.

reports to communicate to our colleagues who may still have some hesitation on the question whether medical gymnastic treatment can work in harmony with bathing-cures. Gentlemen generally attend the medical gymnastic treatment in the early morning in the intervals between taking the waters; ladies devote some time to it later in the morning, without the least inconvenience, notwithstanding the strong baths used with us, as, for instance mud-baths, and the use of strong mineral waters. Therefore, here in Sweden, the conviction of the curative power of gymnastics has passed into the public mind, and no difficulties on the matter remain. We sometimes excuse certain »habitués» who exercise their muscles 7 or 8 months a year but never a patient affected with heart-disease, or a young lady suffering from scoliosis. The reports of Dr. HEILIGENTHAL of Baden-Baden are also remarkable with respect to this. He says, for instance: »The 18th of June 1884 *the division for medico-mechanical Zander Gymnastics* was opened with about 20 apparatus, and after about two years this division was considerably enlarged, so that it now possesses 73 gymnastic apparatus. Its popularity has increased with the enlargement. In 1884, we had 115 subscribers for this special division of Friedrichsbad. This number had increased to 269 in 1885 and to 633 in 1887. Such rapid increase is an indisputable proof of the utility of this new curative method, and the synoptical table which follows [1] of cases that have been treated, shows most distinctly the variety of its use.»

In consequence of the above noted success, Wiesbaden, Wildbad, Aix-la-Chapelle and Ragatz have followed the example of Baden-Baden, where in fact a second complete Institute has lately been founded, as we have already mentioned.

HEILIGENTHAL, as well as NEBEL, HASEBROEK &c. mention in their annual reports and various works a number of cases of particularly serious affections of the heart that they have had under their treatment, and we refer to these works persons who take special interest in the matter.

The Zander method is not in any way limited to diseases of the cardiac muscles which must be ascribed to want of exer-

---

[1] For want of space this table has been omitted. See reports of Dr. Heiligenthal, Baden-Baden.

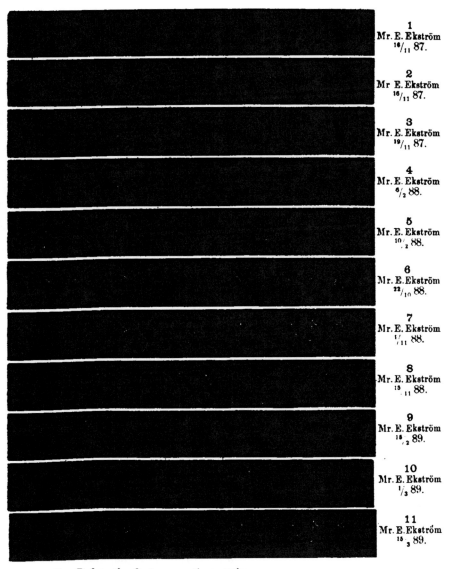

1
Mr. E. Ekström
$^{16}/_{11}$ 87.

2
Mr E. Ekström
$^{16}/_{11}$ 87.

3
Mr. E. Ekström
$^{19}/_{11}$ 87.

4
Mr. E. Ekström
$^{6}/_{2}$ 88.

5
Mr. E. Ekström
$^{10}/_{2}$ 88.

6
Mr. E. Ekström
$^{22}/_{10}$ 88.

7
Mr. E. Ekström
$^{1}/_{11}$ 88.

8
Mr. E. Ekström
$^{15}/_{11}$ 88.

9
Mr. E. Ekström
$^{15}/_{2}$ 89.

10
Mr. E. Ekström
$^{1}/_{3}$ 89.

11
Mr. E. Ekström
$^{15}/_{3}$ 89.

1. Before the first gymnastic exercise.
2. After the first gymnastic exercise.

The subsequent diagrams date from various periods in the course of the exercises.

During the summer of 1888 the patient had no gymnastic treatment.

cise and to abuse of food and drink. On the contrary, the
mechanical treatment can be applied without fear in cases of
valvular lesions of the heart and in diseases of the cardiac
muscles due to excessive fatigue- NEBEL quotes (p. 204) the
opinions of ZANDER on the species of diseases of the heart
treated by him: »He (ZANDER) recommends gymnastics for all
the valvular lesions and their consecutive states, in idiopathic
hypertrophy and dilatation (overwork), chronic myocarditis, fatty
degeneration of the heart, nervous heart troubles, stenocarditis,
nervous palpitations of the heart, arteriosclerosis. He says that
the treatment, when used with perseverance, is always favorable.
He is of opinion that complete *recovery* is obtained only in
cases of simple hypertrophy and incipient fatty degeneration.
He rightly considers as a success for which one ought to be
thankful, the fact that patients affected with incurable diseases
of the heart, find great relief from painful symptoms and even
come so far that, with some modification of their mode of life
and a little caution, they do not experience any inconveniencies
from their diseases.»

For those of our readers who may be inclined to think that
we exaggerate our eulogies of the Zander method, we take the
liberty of giving (p. 61) from our considerable collection of diagrams of the heart-pulsation, taken with the assistance of
DUDGEON's sphygmograph, some proofs that will no doubt
abundantly show the special importance of our treatment,
at least in the case in question.

b. Diseases of the nerves.

There is scarcely any need to say that a great number of
patients with nervous complaints of various kinds frequent our
Institute, and for a large portion of these sufferings, medical
gymnastics no doubt play a most important part, though this
importance may not be so great as for diseases of the heart.
At the risk of classifying our subject incorrectly from the point
of view of pathological anatomy, we begin by the kind of nervous diseases which most frequently present themselves to our
daily treatment. We mean *neurasthenia* and its near relation
hysteria. May we be permitted to quote by way of introduction a few words by Dr. NEBEL: »Persons suffering from *general*

weakness of the nerves and from hysteria can, as Dr. ZANDER assures me, and as my own experience teaches me, derive great advantage from gymnastic treatment, on condition that the evil be not too far advanced, that we may set to work with requisite prudence and patience, and that we succeed in keeping in good spirits the usually rather depressed patients. It is true that the closer the nervous affection approximates to insanity the greater is the difficulty of attaining good results, especially in our establishments.»

Speaking of the importance of medical gymnastics as a dietetic remedy, we have already alluded to a great many causes connected with neurasthenia and also partly with hysteria.

Dr. HASEBROEK has described the principal causes of this real scourge of our times in an excellent pamphlet called: »*On nervosity and want of exercise in large cities.*» [1] He says somewhere: »It is the use of medico-mechanical gymnastics on a large scale that justifies the hygienic importance attributed to the method. In large cities ample occasion is thereby given to the inhabitants to develop their physical and mental health by systematical bodily exercise. Since the foundation of medico-mechanical Institutes, continues the author, a great number of invalids have there sought and found a remedy for nervous affections; the individuals of this category furnish a considerable proportion of patients to the mechanical treatment, and are amongst those from whose care one derives the greatest pleasure. The typical expressions of these patients, that they »*don't know themselves again*», that they »*are new men*» are particularly proper to show the success resulting from the gymnastic treatment. The category of nervous individuals also furnishes the Institute with the majority of regular patients who display an astonishing perseverance; they feel the want of performing every day their self-imposed task of exercises, and devote themselves with ardour and pleasure to them, thanks to which they are armed for daily resistance against the attacks on mind and spirits caused by over-exertion in the struggle for existence.»

Dr. HEILIGENTHAL of Baden-Baden specially draws our attention to the forms complicated by marked disposition to melan-

---

[1] Über die Nervosität und den Mangel an körperlicher Bewegung in der Gross-stadt etc. Hamburg 1891.

choly, and the treatment of which was followed by extraordinary success. Dr. FRIEDMANN of the Institute at Mannheim says: »With very few exceptions the results with these patients have been very good; they decidedly belong to the subjects who are most susceptible to gymnastic treatment.» Dr. NEBEL is less positive in his hopes than his colleagues. He does, however, justly appreciate the importance of medical gymnastic treatment and he says (p. 106): »Now and then we receive visitors who do not abandon themselves to exaggerated hopes, patients who have felt, themselves, that systematical exercises taken regularly have a good influence on their general well-being and on the suppression of their weakness.» In another place he says, speaking of these patients: »A great many of them show much gratitude. Several of them have become warm partisans of the Zander system, *which has made new men of them.*» Our experience during a long succession of years confirms the above. We must not conceal, however, that our treatment has often stranded on the want of perseverance in the patient. We cannot too often and too strongly insist on this inconvenience which, more than the insufficiency of our treatment, paralyses our efforts. This circumstance surprises us the less in neurasthenia, as want of perseverance and energy is exactly the characteristic feature of this disease; this weakness of will often hinders the patient from pursuing the treatment to the end, and induces him to incessantly try new methods of treatment. The family physician ought, more than is generally the case, to take the part of gymnastics and support them vigorously by trying to make the patient understand how much his well-being depends on a conscientious use of the treatment, and not on a planless passing from one curative method to another. What a power of persuasion we need for the purpose of hindering the patient from abandoning the treatment after the first feeble and delusive signs of a temporary improvement, or when, after a few months, discontent takes hold of him and he wrongly fancies that the desired improvement will never take place.

The first symptom on which our treatment works, is *sleeplessness*. In all cases where it has not been of long continuance, there is undeniably no better remedy than medical gymnastics, which better than any other treatment are able to reduce the employment of narcotics. Unfortunately it is often not till these remedies have been long and vainly used that the patient trusts himself to our treatment. The effect of the latter is to improve the circulation of the blood, to facilitate the assimilation of the food and thus to increase the physical and moral power of resistance. When neurasthenia appears under the form of nervous *excitement*, this power of resistance is noticeable by a diminution of general irritability; when in the form of nervous *depression*, by an increase of elasticity of body and finally by all the ›turgescence of life› (*turgor vitœ*). But this cannot be attained without long treatment, especially as many of the predisposing causes often continue to exist, and we have no weapon against them, for the reason that they are to be found in the occupations, the social position or the domestic relations of the patient. Provided the requisite time is given to the treatment, there will not be any later necessity for the patient to abandon totally his ordinary occupations; he may have but to distribute his work more equally and to more strictly observe the dietetic prescriptions. For a great number of patients this point is of an importance not to be neglected, for there are very few persons whose social position is such as to exempt them from all work, all anxiety for the necessities of life, and allow of their devoting themselves exclusively to the maintenance of their health. As we have said, brilliant success is reserved for gymnastics in this domain, and it will be obtained when the patient has at his side a physician who emphasises the value of our system in the interest of the patient, or when we treat patients intelligent enough to understand themselves the great benefits they derive from energetically continuing the treatment to the end.

Another symptom often accompanied by neurasthenia is *cephalalgia* with a sensation of *vacuity* or of *heaviness of the head*. Cephalalgia can, it is true, be due to some affection of the brain or of the stomach. Sometimes it is the faithful attendant of chlorosis and anæmia; often also the origin is to be sought in the rheumatic infiltrations of the neck-muscles (myitis), one of the most frequent causes of cephalalgia. In many analogous cases medical gymnastics can be used advantageously, combined with massage and electricity. In infiltrations of the

5

66

neck-muscles it will always be necessary to use massage before, or simultaneously with, gymnastics. In cephalalgia the chief thing is to find the affected muscles of the neck and temples and to give special attention to the ramifications of the trigeminal nerve.

We will be brief regarding the other nervous diseases.

In *epilepsy*, for instance, gymnastics, and especially derivative [1] movements would no doubt have a highly beneficial influence. But it is indeed difficult, if not entirely impossible to treat at our Institutes, persons affected with this disease, for who can guarantee that one of the attacks does not occur in the course of the treatment; a single attack would be of a nature to cause general excitement among the other patients present and might be excessively distressing and even dangerous to them. These patients therefore ought rather to take their movements at home and by manual treatment.

Medical gymnastics, on the contrary show brilliant results with respect to *chorea*. Dr. NEBEL quotes ZANDER's opinion on the matter: »He (ZANDER) recommends the treatment of chorea by movements, as being particularly effective and, in all cases, leading to recovery after three months; by not affecting the organism as does a large portion of the medicine we take, it gives the patient greater power of resistance and, consequently, protects him against relapses. ZANDER considers as the object of the treatment, the improvement of the muscular innervation by the use of regular and more varied, (*but by no means specific*) movements which ought not to be too strong, but which are frequently repeated, and regulated so that the stimulation and effect of our treatment are distributed over as wide regions of innervation as possible.

Let us pass now to the essential diseases of the nerves. A great number of neuralgic complaints are often treated at our Institute with most satisfactory results, especially when we meet with palpable changes generally due to rheumatic myitis. The action of the nerves is subjected to changes by the effect of pressure of the swollen muscular mass on the trunks of nerves, or by the spreading of the inflammation to the sheath of the nerves. Our investigation has for object to discover these myitis

[1] In medical gymnastics we call derivative movements those that have for their object to produce a flow of blood to the periferic parts.

and to remove, by massage and gymnastic movements, these changes in the muscles and nerves. It is in these cases ZANDER's vibration-movements play an important part, and as soon as their utility was understood, various apparatus were invented such as GRANVILLE's and LIEDBÄCK's[1] vibrators. The importance of these isolated forms of movement is too slight, when it is not combined with general treatment which ought not and is not intended to exclude local treatment.

Paralysis is also an object of gymnastic treatment. Here, the desired end can only be attained by great patience, unfailing energy, and to a certain degree by a special disposition for such work. The limited time of the physician, however, is too precious to be devoted to purely mechanical work, the monotony of which puts the greatest perseverance to a severe test. We are therefore compelled to restrict ourselves to the supervision of the treatment, entrusting the patients to the care of the gymnast. In that case, we choose by preference women-assistants, for these, as a rule, possess an admirable tenacity and energy, and their efforts are rewarded with almost miraculous success. It is scarcely needful to say that we do not willingly allow these patients to use our apparatus during the ordinary time of treatment, considering that they hinder the exercises of other patients. Besides they require incessant supervision, and often the paralysis appears under such forms that they cannot make use of certain apparatus, in consequence of the particular construction of the latter. These patients, therefore, ought to be treated at special hours, which would be reserved for them. The natural result is that our gymnastics become very expensive for them, and, for this reason, we prefer in Sweden, as a rule, to employ principally manual gymnastics given at home in the treatment of such diseases. A certain ingenuity is required, however, in these cases to determine the initial position and at the same time invent in special cases the particular movements suitable for them. It is therefore easy to see that here also, there is need of intelligence and dexterity combined with perseverance and strength to work.

---

[1] These two apparatus have no doubt their value in *local* treatment, but they can neither give as *strong* vibrations, nor affect *simultaneously such large parts of the body* as the Zander apparatus, wherefore it is but natural that they cannot substitute them.

68

We have spoken above of women-gymnasts and we hasten
to add that we have often witnessed the success they are able
to realise in *infantile spinal paralysis* or *myelitis of the anterior
cornua of the spinal cord*, the treatment of which sometimes
requires a long series of years.

Writer's cramp and other allied professional neuroses offer
a no less favorable field for gymnastic treatment, if one has
really to do with a peripheral origin of the disease, and if one
succeeds in discovering here and there in the muscles the affected
points sensitive to pressure in connection with the writer's incorrect position, and also in cases where over-exertion of certain
nerves and groups of muscles have caused this enfeeblement. It is
to be highly recommended to combine gymnastic treatment with
massage' and *pressure on the trunks of the nerves*, a form of movement very frequently employed in manual gymnastics and which
may have great success in the hands of an experienced gymnast.

Every director of a medical gymnastic Institute will also
find himself obliged to receive among his patients a certain
number of persons suffering from diseases of the *spinal cord*.
It is equally possible to attain a successful result in certain
kinds of these diseases. Dr. NEBEL (ibid., page 314) enumerates:
anæmia and hyperæmia of the spinal cord, the consequences
of spinal apoplexy, chronic myelitis &c.

As regards the posterior spinal sclerosis or »locomotor ataxia»
(*tabes dorsalis*), opinions widely differ with respect to gymnastic treatment for this disease. Some physicians recommend it,
while others reject it. It is probable that the truth, here as in
many cases, is to be found between these two diametrically
opposed opinions. Medical gymnastics cannot on any account
do the patient any harm, and a suitable and careful treatment
would always be of symptomatic use. I fully share Dr. NEBEL's
opinion when he says: »The symptomatic relief, the temporary
improvement can be produced by gymnastic treatment, as well
as by electro-hydrotherapeutics and frequentation of baths.» Whoever has some knowledge of the anatomical condition of these
patients will not consider a *restitutio ad integrum* possible,
either by vibration of the nerves as employed by Mr. KJELLGREN
or by any other method. We often hear accounts of occurring
improvements, especially by the director, Mr. KJELLGREN, and

his disciples. The explanation is easy enough for the initiate, considering that this disease, often without any treatment at all, comes to a stand-still and even shows *apparent* improvement, while the result is always the same.

At all events, medical gymnastics will show equally good results with all other treatments in use.

Regarding *infantile spinal paralysis*, we are convinced that simultaneous use of massage, gymnastics and electricity would be most advantageous. [1] »As soon as the acute symptoms have disappeared» says Dr. Kleen, »the sooner massage be applied, the greater is the prospect of keeping the muscles and other affected parts in a better state of nutrition, and of limiting deformities.» In this twofold respect, the treatment is of a prophylactic importance, which is not to be despised. We cannot but mention that we have observed several cases where mothers have acquired a certain degree of skill in gymnastics, and have treated their children themselves; they continued indefatigably for years, as mothers alone can do, and in some cases the result can be looked upon as being exceedingly successful. We do not think we can conclude this subject better than by the following words of Dr. Nebel: »It is our firm conviction that our curative proceeding, always useful and never injurious, demanding little preparation and expense, gives us the most effective means for preventing and arresting secondary progressive disorders in the distribution of the blood, the regulation of the heat, and in the nutrition, the development and utility of the injured member as well as for the entire bodily condition.

What has been said of infantile, spinal paralysis is equally applicable to the *paralysis due to hemorrhage of the brain*. The principal point is not to lose courage. With persevering treatment and the help of nature one generally attains to a supportable condition.

We have reviewed systematically a series of nervous diseases and have shown that we can also contribute our mite towards the treatment of these diseases generally so void of consolation.

---

[1] We must not forget that in certain cases it is absolutely necessary to give the little patient a bandage, which, in combination with the means indicated above, produces satisfactory results.

c. Diseases of the respiratory organs.

After this rather detailed description of diseases of the heart
and nerves we will pass rapidly over the other internal diseases,
stopping only to note some important peculiarities.

Concerning the diseases of the *respiratory organs*, our gymnastics have not, it is true, for their morbid affections, as much
importance as for diseases of the heart; but in the first place
they are not contra-indicated and in the second may become
very valuable as a co-operating factor in the medical treatment.

We will first make mention of the vibration of the larynx,
which can be most effective in slight *laryngitis* as well as for
hoarseness and husky voice, and which, according to Dr. Nebel,
exercises an agreeable and beneficial effect after much speaking
and singing. In chronic bronchial catarrh, the effect of our inter-
vention is to improve the circulation in the thorax and in the
periphery of the body, as well as vigorously to promote the
contraction of the involuntary muscles of the bronchiæ, and
thereby to facilitate the expectoration. In this case dorsal vibration
plays a great part in the treatment.

The same effect is arrived at in *bronchial asthma* by movements tending to promote the circulation and principally by
vibration-movements on the back. On the majority of our patients, our curative means work as specifics, and especially as
specifics that can be tried without the least danger.

The diseases of the pulmonary tissues are so far accessible
to our treatment, as it causes a more complete ventilation of
the lungs, the dilatation of the thorax, and systematically
strengthens the respiratory muscles. »According to the choice
and distribution of movements, one can render more complete
either the inspiration or expiration.»[1]

Medical gymnastics can also be useful in pulmonary emphy-
sema, for these patients derive no advantage from their thorax being
compressed by exterior means; they ought rather to learn how to
breathe deeply and to be able themselves to ventilate their lungs.
In tuberculosis of the lungs the greatest caution must be observed;
one must keep almost exclusively to derivative movements and to

[1] Nebel ibid.

such as exercise a generally strengthening influence, in order to act, in a way, indirectly on the lungs, and the direct respiratory movements should be avoided, at least in the beginning.

d. Diseases of the abdominal organs.

Medical gymnastics exercise on the diseases of the abdominal organs an influence, the value of which it would be wrong not to appreciate sufficiently. Dr. NEBEL says most judiciously on this subject, that massage on the abdomen here predominates to such a degree, that other, not less important indications are totally left aside, namely to revive *the sunken vital energy* and to stimulate the various organs and systems to greater activity. In giving massage, it is overlooked that the movements of the body are the simplest and most natural means for restoring the disturbed equilibrium in the economy of the body. By bringing into activity the muscles of the abdomen, the weakening of these muscles as well as of those of the stomach and intestines is prevented, and we try to counteract by our treatment the abnormal processes of digestion which result in dilatation of the stomach. By strengthening the muscles of the abdomen, we stimulate the peristaltic movement, we struggle against the atony of the intestinal viscera, and finally we facilitate the discharge of the excrements.

Massage of the abdomen will always conserve, however, its great value; the effect is also excellent when the object is to act temporarily upon the atony of the intestinal canal and incite it to action, but, it constitutes by no means the single and exclusive method, for it receives its predominant importance and lasting effect only by judiciously given gymnastics. »There has broken out», says Dr. NEBEL with infinite reason, »a real mania for abdomen-massage, and the worst of it is that frequently the practice of massage is confided to intruders and ignorant people to whom the strength of the kneading is the principal thing and the manner of the application a matter of no consequence. It is possible that this proceeding in most cases brings on a temporary improvement, but it can be only of limited effect and can certainly not have the complex effect of gymnastics.» —

»The kneading represents an often indispensable aid, but not in any way the chief factor in the treatment of an affection which, rationally, ought to be attacked, not in its local manifestation, but in its deeper causes, not only in the abdomen, but in the whole body of the patient.»

For many years we have combined, in our Institutes, gymnastics, massage and the prescription of various mineral waters, such as those of Karlsbad, Marienbad, Kissingen &c., and we have ever had to note the best success. We are convinced also that, many a time, treatment at bathing-establishments would offer more satisfactory, more lasting results, if *the water-cure were combined with a rational movement-cure.*

It is this system which really is the rule at our Swedish bathing-places, and the additional expense that gymnastics involve, is comparatively of little importance.

Let us point out the importance of abdomen-vibration to the height of the umbilicus in *chronic intestinal catarrh* with diarrhæa, and all our kneading-movements in *ordinary constipation.* We refer those who take a special interest in these questions, to Dr. NEBEL's work, where the general treatment has been minutely described. We had better add perhaps that many patients experience a deterioration in their condition during the first days; but there is no reason for uneasiness, as that will pass off after a few weeks.

We know that *hemorrhoids* are chiefly due to blood-stoppings in the veins, and we usually contend with success against the slighter forms of this evil. Pelvis-elevation (E 8) is a form of movement to be recommended as it has always proved beneficial; that is also the case with sacrum-vibration. It would not enter any physician's head to employ only gymnastics in a *chronic catarrh of the bladder*, but, in combination with medicinal treatment, the patient finds relief by certain movements and especially by massage. Dr. WIDE, director of the Orthopedic Institute in Stockholm, has gained rich experience on this matter, which he will soon give to the public.

In connection with the preceding we will say a few words on the treatment of the *diseases of women.* It is by no means our intention to place our gymnastic method in competition with massage of the pelvis, so much in vogue at the present moment. But »Brandt's [1] treatment» involves a great many active movements of resistance, as well as combined operations which can be given with equal advantage at our Institutes, and which thus spare the specialists the fatigue of personal exercise. Let us add that we increase, in an extraordinary way, the general well-being of the patient which naturally has a favorable influence on the local affection.

In *disorders of the menstruation* we cannot say enough for the excellence of our treatment, the efficiency of which we have had occasion to observe during a long series of years, and regarding which manual gymnastics have also great sucess to record.

Finally, may we be allowed to repeat here, by way of conclusion, Dr. Zander's words on the importance of gymnastics during pregnancy: »A selected number of muscle-exercises, executed with carefulness are of great use during pregnancy, because of their beneficial influence on the general state of health. Repeated observations have shown that, owing to a preparation of this kind, *parturition* has been easier than in previous cases, when gymnastic treatment had not been used.» We will add that in the descent of the uterus (*prolapsus uteri*), Dr. Zander has communicated to us most remarkable results, obtained by the special movements E 8, B 5b, as well as by vibration of the lumbar region.

e. Constitutional anomalies.

Gymnastic treatment has also proved efficient in *anæmia* and *chlorosis*, though generally in combination with ferruginous remedies and mineral waters of various kinds. The effect of our treatment is first noticed by the disappearance of various symptoms of the disease, such as cephalalgia, sensitiveness of the epigastrium, coldness of hands and feet, pains in the back and legs, general weariness &c.

A rational treatment, carefully superintended, produces, in the struggle against these symptoms, a most satisfactory improvement in the general health: the distribution of the blood be-

---

[1] Since many years one of our prominent gymnasts, Major Brandt, has treated sucessfully various diseases of women by massage as well as by gymnastics.

comes more equal, the nutrition improves, and the curative effect manifests itself in an increased weight of body and a healthier appearance.

f. Obesity.

Corpulent persons frequently attend our Institutes. The diminution of the periphery of the body is often very considerable, owing to the systematical use of our apparatus, in combination with a strict observation of a suitable regimen. NEBEL makes on this subject a few remarks to which we give our full approval: »With mechanical gymnastics we can come to the assistance of all our corpulent people; without exposing them to any danger, we can treat ladies with very weak muscles and who are so very indolent that a short walk on level ground is a great trouble to them, as well as asthmatic gentlemen with very weak hearts.

»There are often seen patients who, after losing ·16 lbs. or 20 lbs. of their weight by »mountain-climbing», or at Karlsbad, Marienbad, Kissingen &c., soon re-acquire their former corpulence on returning to their own homes where they soon relapse into their old habits.» — »It would indeed be quite easy,» adds NEBEL »to guard against this inconvenience, if people would employ gymnastics as additional treatment after their return from the baths.»

Professor ÅBERG, former director of the Medico-mechanical Institute at Buenos-Ayres, says: »The desired end is generally attained, and ascertained by the balance. Still I have observed that the balance is not sufficient for controlling the treatment in a satisfactory way. Muscular exercises serve, as we know, to form new muscular fibres, which can even slightly increase the weight of the body, considering that flesh is heavier than fat. The consumption of fat is effected in the soft parts of the body, in the omentum and the covering of the intestines, where the fat causes the chief inconveniences. The volume of the abdomen may diminish without the body's losing its total weight.»

Vigorous movements are not advisable, for a large proportion of the patients cannot support them. Some corpulent patients find it convenient to give up an hour a day to exercise, and then not to be obliged to submit to restraint of any kind in

their easy and irregular mode of life. ZANDER utters the following remarkable words in a letter to Dr. NEBEL: »I have also fat
and corpulent patients who grow thin with excessive slowness;
but what is to be done when they are incapable of giving up
sugar, farinaceous food and the consumption of too much drink?»

Dr. NEBEL gives on this circumstance the following strikingly
true opinion: »Obese persons have every reason to be thankful,
if we succeed in diminishing their increase of volume. The patient becomes more mobile, gets rid of his troublesome palpitations of the heart, of his difficulty of breathing, of his sudden
weariness, of his disposition to catarrhs, and all this by means
of a treatment that does not enfeeble the body, but strengthens
it, hardens it against possible dangers, and makes it in every
respect more fit to do its functions. Compared to these advantages it is of little matter if the weight of the body be a few
pounds more or less, provided, as we said, it is possible to prevent further increase of weight.

g. Gout.

Gout cannot be cured either by gymnastics or baths, but a
cure may possibly be effected by their combination with a general,
medicinal, and especially dietetic, treatment. The movements are,
however, of great prophylactic importance and almost prevent the
attacks of gout. Gouty people employ, by preference, our gymnastic method which, according to their own declarations, contributes
to their wellbeing. We have often treated with massage and especially with »effleurage» acute attacks of gout, and we have frequently succeeded in shortening the crisis, so called. An invalid
very nearly related to us, our own father, suffered from gout for
20 years and was thus treated; he was not compelled to keep
his bed, he managed his medical practice and died at the age
of 77. This result was not attained, it is true, but by an
»effleurage» very slight in the beginning, but often lasting 15
or 20 minutes. We believe that this treatment effectively sup-
ports the general treatment, and that, besides, gout is very much
more common in Sweden than we believe, considering that in its
mildest forms we usually see a chronic rheumatism; it is not
until a renal colic or an attack of podagra makes the situation
clear, that we can make a sure diagnosis.

76

h. Chronic rheumatism of the articulations.

The difference between gout and chronic rheumatism of the articulations is undoubtedly very great both in origin and in symptoms. These two diseases have nevertheless many symptoms in common, and therefore our points of attack are partly the same in the two cases. Patients affected with the one or the other consequently in summer seek bathing-places offering various kinds of baths, and in winter, employ massage and gymnastic treatment. When it is possible to find out inflammatory alterations (myitis) of the muscles, these usually become objects of thorough and careful massage. Often these muscular affections are not limited to small centres, but the practised hand of the »masseur» soon discovers the abnormal quality of the muscle, which is soft and pasty to the touch and wanting in normal elasticity. Hardnesses also appear round and in the articulations, as also at the insertion-points of the muscles. In these cases the first indication is to give massage to the affected parts, a proceeding which is generally crowned with a certain success. — »Therefore one always made use of active movements acting on the affected muscle, of gentle, passive movements of some duration, accompanied by »effleurage», rubbings, percussions, beatings, strokings, sawings, kneadings, vibrations, in a word, of all the mechanical operations which, under the name of massage, are introduced as a new branch of science» (NEBEL p. 333).

The history of such movements goes as far back as 200 years, therefore to a period very much anterior to that when the renowned METZGER of Amsterdam systematised them to a certain degree. A proof of this fact is particularly furnished by our Swedish bathing-place of Loka, [1] where patients are rubbed with cold mud, after a pail of tepid water has been poured over them. This kind of baths known in Sweden since the year 1727 by a work of Dr. VICTORIN, was in a way, already employed, traditionally, half a century before this epoch. For all these questions we refer to a work by Dr. KLEEN on *massage* (see p. 12).

We consider that massage without simultaneous or consecutive gymnastic treatment is but an incomplete work. May we

[1] See work: »Emploi de la vase dans les Bains de mer de Suède» par le Dr. HENRI DOR, Paris 1861.

be permitted to quote, in support of our argument the following
words of ZANDER to which we give our full approval and which
are based on the results of a rich experience in these matters:
»We must therefore keep in mind that massage, the object of
which is to free the swollen tissues from abnormal infiltrations and morbid dispositions, and which consequently should
be considered as a process of purification, cannot alone be able
to restore an organ (muscle, articulation) to the normal, vigorous
state; gymnastic exercises are also necessary for the attainment
of this result. Massage, without gymnastics, is an incomplete
treatment which, as we understand, has been continued by certain individuals for many years without any other benefit than
temporary improvement. It is in reality an abuse of the massage
which must not, however, always be attributed exclusively to
the ignorance or incapacity of the masseur, as it is also often
due to the laziness of the patient, who prefers being kneaded
by another to making the necessary movements himself.»

On the other hand, we will openly confess that we have
not always been successful in our treatment of gout and rheumatism by gymnastics alone, but have prescribed massage as a
treatment of recognised efficiency. Massage is given therefore
every day and every hour at our Swedish gymnastic Institutes.
These diseases often leave behind them stiffness of one or more
articulations, and numbers of such cases present themselves in
our practice. May we again be permitted to quote NEBEL's opinion on this subject (ibid., p. 330): »The Zander apparatus are
applicable in all these cases; some amongst them, as for instance
those intended for arm-movements, can be adjusted at any angle,
in accordance with the deformity of the affected articulation;
all allow of a cautious and exactly measurable effect as regards
the rotation *and the degree of effort required.* Suppose that
we have to make supple some stiffened articulation, the shoulder
for instance. Any one who, as a medical assistant at an hospital,
has had to give necessary passive movements, will remember
the anguish with which children and women especially watched
our preparations. How much more simply and rationally we
set about it now, employing Dr. ZANDER's apparatus A 7.
Arm-rolling either passively by fastening the hand and the
arm to the horizontal bar by means of straps, or actively by

fastening the shoulder in the crutch by similar means. At first we describe a very small circle; the patient experiences little or no pain and goes to his exercises without anxiety. We enlarge the circle only by slow degrees, almost insensibly from N° 1 to N° 20, never giving more than the inevitable pain. We work passively with a very slight use of strength, compared to the considerable and useless exertion we used before to overcome the resistance opposed, not by the disease, but by the involuntary tension of the muscles of the patient. Very soon we utilise for our end the strength of the patient himself who must move the lever alternately backwards and forwards. Many times after rheumatic affections and very often after stiffness in the shoulder brought on by its inactivity due to the arm's being carried in a sling for some length of time, I have been able to make the articulations supple after a period of 5 or 6 weeks by the most gentle proceeding; as a matter of course I do not speak of a complete cure, unless the shoulder-blade remain in its place when I lift the arm; the contrary is the rule, as we know, in affections of the shoulders. The various apparatus serving to move the articulations, equally facilitate our work: E 2 for passive hand-flexion and extension, E 3 for passive hand-adduction and abduction, B 12 for foot-rolling &c.

»All the other apparatus can in different ways help us to attain our end, provided we know how to use them ingeniously, and do not look for prescriptions and patterns, nor seek apparatus for each special purpose, but exert ourselves to find the suitable treatment for each special case.» — The celebrated orthopedist Dr Nebel also speaks most justly of the apparatus invented and constructed on the Zander system by Dr. Hönig of Breslau for the purpose of bending and extending the forearm; he says: »They are not only a *superfluous expense* but also *dangerously violent means*. Similar apparatus are of so little *practical need* that we are obliged to see in such a wish for *superfluous* inventions, immediate danger to our cause.»

VIII.

The Zander Gymnastics in the service of Workmens' Insurance.

The Zander gymnastic method has obtained, in the course of the last few years, an application undoubtedly of a nature to extend hereafter its sphere of activity over an ever widening field and to make it a real necessity for the civilized world. We mean its employment in the service of industrial corporations or syndicates. These institutions being, to a certain extent, foreign to other countries than Germany, we deem it right to explain more particularly their origin and their object.

There have long existed in Germany, as well as in other countries, a great number of Trades-Associations, founded for the object of studying and defending the mutual, professional interest of their members. But, properly speaking, it is from the year 1884, and in consequence of an Act promulgated at this period, for the protection of workmen from the consequences of accidents occurring in the course of their work, that these Associations have developed under a new form, that of ›Workmen's Insurance against Accidents».

The 1st Article of this German Act is of the following purport:

›Persons who work for wages:

›1:o. In mines, salt-works, works for mechanical preparation of ores, in stone-quarries and gravel-pits, in manufactories and works, on railways or river steam-navigation, in wharves and dock-yards;

›2:o. In trades and other sedentary industrial and commercial professions;

›3:o. In manufactories where steam-boilers or engines driven by mechanical force are made use of &c. &c. —

should be insured, according to the prescription of the present Act against the consequences of accidents occurring in the course of their work.›

»When the accident does not involve death, the indemnity consists in the payment of medical treatment from the 14th week[1] and in payment to the injured of sick-pay which lasts as long as his incapacity for work. The sick-pay is calculated according to the average wages of the injured up to 4 »marks» (shillings); above that sum the surplus is only counted by one thirds.

»This pension consists:

»In cases of total incapacity for work and for the duration of this incapacity, of sixty-six and two thirds per cent of his wages.

»In cases of partial incapacity and for the duration of this incapacity, in a fraction of the above pension, calculated according to the remaining ability to work.»

For further details we refer to the work of M. AMEDÉE MARTEAU, (see note[2]). In consequence of the prescriptions of the Act which also place the superintendence and organisation of these Insurances against Accidents in the hands of the Associations above mentioned, there actually exist in Germany 112 Corporations or *Trades-Associations*, which include above 13 $1/_2$ millions of workmen. The principal object is, as we see, to assist the workman to regain his capacity for work and thereby to enable him to support himself and his family.

This task belongs, it is true, in the first place to the hospitals, which naturally are first called upon to take care of the injured.

Hospitals have also the task to limit to the smallest possible degree the immediate consequences of the accident. But, the after-treatment, which in most cases is of so great importance from the point of view of future capacity for work, must generally take place outside the hospital. Considering the organisation of the hospitals and the small accomodation in proportion to the number of accidents, it is evident that all the patients do receive their discharge as speedily as

---

[1] For the preceding time the sick relief funds have, according to the Act of 13th of June 1883, the obligation to help the sick or injured.

[2] Les Assurances ouvrières en Allemagne. Rapport adressé à M. le Ministre des Affaires Étrangères par M. Amédée Marteau, Consul de France. Paris. Ch. Leroy. 1887.

possibie in order to give room to others. The patient is indeed, on leaving the hospital, cured of his injuries, but in most cases he is entirely incapable of work. The after-treatment, the importance of which we have already pointed out, must therefore be confided to other persons, and in the first place to the physician belonging to the Association. But this physician is generally not well remunerated, his time is taken up by private practice, and besides, he has not at his disposal the special arrangements without which such work rarely shows favorable results. He must therefore in most cases surrender this after-treatment to professional »masseurs», to *barber-surgeons* &c. who usually possess neither the intelligence nor the knowledge requisite for using this difficult work to advantage.

»The co-operation of a patient», continues the German colleague, from whom we borrowed the above lines and who has also much occupied himself with this matter, »to whom it has been prescribed to exercise his injured limbs in a certain way, naturally leaves much to be desired. The treatment is lengthened proportionally, and very frequently the time when good results might have been obtained is allowed to pass. The anchylosis of the articulations, the contraction of ligaments and capsules, the atrophy of muscles, and paralysis, have often been the consequences of injuries. All these sad results would probably have been avoided, if the numerous remedies offered by gymnastics had been employed in time. The medico-mechanical Institutes are in the first place called upon to remedy the mentioned inconveniences in the after-treatment of the injured, and to satisfy a want so long and deeply felt by physicians and patients. That they can do so is owing to their arrangements described in the preceding pages and to their technically instructed personnel which, without being exclusively medical, is, however, under continual superintendence of physicians. The patients belonging to these Associations, have promptly recognised the advantages of our Institutes, and, wherever these have been founded, lively and continued relations between them and the patients in question have immediately been developed. The experience gained in this respect can be considered most satisfactory. A great number of patients disabled by accidents, some of them receiving sick-pay for many years, have been enabled to resume their occupations, either altogether or partially. The result has been most clearly manifested where mechanical treatment was begun before the development of the secondary symptoms mentioned above. This experience has led the Associations to make the justifiable decision, to employ, in suitable cases, this treatment from the end of the prescribed 13 weeks after the accident.»

In the rare cases where treatment at the Institute has not succeeded in producing an improvement, it has nevertheless been of use to the Associations. Thanks to the exact clinical reports that have been furnished, they have been able to estimate with greater certainty the larger or smaller amount of indemnity that they were bound to pay.

»With the Zander apparatus it is possible to apply more or less resistance without the patient's perceiving it. In two cases the presence of deceit has been proved by means of the graduated lever. One result for the Associations is of course the greater security against attempts at fraud by pensioners dreading work.

»The expense of gymnastic treatment can scarcely be taken into consideration, compared to the great majority of cases in which increased capacity for work has been obtained. The question is really of an initial expense, doing away with the obligation for the Association for *years*. But indepedently of this financial side of the question, the influence on the workman of his increased ability to work, is so fruitful in good results that one finds ample reward for expense and trouble. We have often seen in our patients that the feeling of incapacity to provide for the wants of their families and of depression at the sight of the gradual decline of their economical circumstances, gave room to a feeling of assurance and gratitude at the return of their strength and ability to work.»

We have said that workmen disabled by accidents are generally compelled to apply to incompetent persons for aftertreatment. But as a rule that is not the case in Sweden, for at the Royal Central Institute, patients are treated gratuitously by the students under the control of Professors. That is equally the case at the Dispensaries of the Hospitals where the greater number of medical assistants and students are bound to learn the principles of massage and gymnastic treatment. We also, at our Medico-mechanical Institutes, and at the Orthopedic Institute, have a considerable number of non-paying patients of this kind. One of our German colleagues whom we have quoted above, Dr. SCHÜTZ, director of the Medico-mechanical Institute of Berlin, has made great and energetic efforts for the development of this after-treatment on a rational basis. He derived assistance no doubt from the dearly bought experience of the Associations i. e. from the considerable number of invalids' pensions that they had paid. This experience was gained by the results of faulty after-treatment, of indifference or want of goodwill in the patients &c. &c. The Associations consequently understood that it was necessary to do something for placing the after-treatment under the care and control of skilled persons. Thanks chiefly to the initiative of Dr. SCHÜTZ, there has been founded at Nieder-Schönhausen, near Berlin, the first Convalescent Home for Workmen disabled by accidents occurring in the course of their work. We borrow from the first report of Dr. SCHÜTZ the following pages on the organisation of the establishment and on the results obtained by the treatment, and we take the liberty of communicating them to our English colleagues.

»*The Convalescent Home* for workmen disabled by accidents (Heimstätte für Verletzte) was established in consequence of a treaty concluded between the president of the cab-owners' corporation and the director of the Medico-mechanical Institute of Berlin. It is the first establishment for the after-treatment of workmen injured in the course of their work, placed under the administration of an Association; it owes its foundation to the ever more urgent wants of a corporation whose members are exposed to numerous and serious accidents in the course of their work.

»The increasing number of pensioners, the increasing amount of the sick-pay, the considerable number of incomplete recoveries caused the leaders of the corporations to give their attention most particularly to the progress of medical science in this domain. The founding of the »Convalescent Home for the Injured» has given a very simple solution to this *desideratum*. The practical accomplishment was rendered possible by various

favorable circumstances and chiefly by the intelligent, combined
action of energetic and disinterested men.

»In close communication with Berlin, and yet removed from
the injurious influences of a large city, the Home is situated in
the midst of gardens of an area of three or four acres, and has,
in a fine building of two stories, bright, healthy rooms for about
50 or 60 patients. In addition to the halls and bed-rooms, the
house contains a large gymnasium, a room for massage, a consulting-room, rooms for a medical assistant, a steward, two masseurs and an engineer; a room for the motor with work-shop,
and finally, kitchen, laundry, bath-room and cellars.

»In the gymnasium, situated on the ground-floor, there are
37[1] original Zander apparatus manufactured in Stockholm under the control of the inventor, for active and passive movements as well as for mechanical operations.

I. Apparatus for active movements.

1. A 1. Arm-sinking.
2. A 2. Arm-raising.
3. A 3. Arm-pulling-downwards.
4. A 4. Arm-stretching-upwards.
5. A 5. Arm-adduction.
6. A 6. Arm-abduction.
7. A 7. Arm-rolling (circumduction).
8. A 8 a. Arm-rotation (active).
9. A 8 b. Arm-rotation (active-passive).
10. A 9. Forearm-flexion.
11. A 10. Forearm-extension.
12. A 11. Hand-flexion and extension.
13. A 12. Finger-flexion and extension.
14. B 3. Hip-knee-flexion.
15. B 4. Hip-knee-extension.
16. B 5 a. Leg-adduction.
17. B 6. Leg-abduction.
18. B 7. Velocipede-motion.

---

[1] At present the Home possesses one more apparatus, namely E 4,
Finger-flexion and extension (passive).

19. B 8. Leg-rotation.
20. B 9. Knee-flexion.
21. B 10. Knee-extension.
22. B 11. Foot-flexion and extension.
23. B 12. Foot-rolling.
24. C 1. Trunk-flexion (sitting).
25. C 2. Trunk-extension (sitting).
26. C 10. Neck-extension.
27. D 3. Trunk-rolling (saddle-sitting).

II. Apparatus for passive movements.

28. E 2. Hand-flexion and extension (passive).
29. E 3. Hand-adduction and abduction (passive).
30. E 6. Chest-expansion.

III. Apparatus for mechanical operations.

31. F 1. Vibration.
32. G 1. Percussion.
33. G 3. Leg-percussion.
34. G 4. Trunk-percussion.
35. I. 1. Arm-rubbing.
36. I. 3. Leg-rubbing.
37. I. 4. Foot-rubbing.

»A side-room, communicating with the gymnasium is intended for *manual gymnastics* (passive movements and resistance-movements) and for *massage*, given, under continual supervision and direction, by the assistants of the Home. Particular attention is given to massage as being an important factor in definite success. The *electric treatment*, by constant or induced current, takes place in the consulting-room. In the spacious underground bath-room, hot, salt baths can be had, if need be. The course of the treatment, generally given twice a day (morning and evening, Sundays and holidays excepted, when the treatment is limited to the morning), is the following:

»The patients repair simultaneously in small parties to the gymnasium, where each receives his *list of movements*, on which are indicated, in a certain order, determined beforehand, the movements or mechanical operations which he has himself to execute, or to receive. Besides the number of the apparatus, the list indicates the degree of resistance, and the length of time the apparatus should be used. The assistants of the establishment take special care that in the exercises the apparatus be employed correctly and thoroughly by the patients.

»After the exercises with the apparatus follow massage and manual gymnastics, and also, for certain patients, electric treatment, as well as the examinations, measurements &c. necessary to complete the sick-journal. The physician, belonging to the establishment, who is always present, superintends the modifications and regulations of the apparatus made necessary by the increase of strength. Lately the application of orthopedic splints (for extension of crooked fingers for instance) has been commenced, and all the splints are manufactured at the workshop of the Home.

»After the morning treatment the patients repair to the halls or the garden of the establishment, where they do their share of the house-work and gardening, but only in the measure prescribed or permitted by the physician in each individual case. A library, well supplied by gifts from friends of the Home, serves for the recreation and instruction of the patients; various games (cards, draughts &c.) and opportunities for smoking in the garden and on the balconies, help to shorten time.

»After their siesta they pass a second time to the mechanical treatment which takes place as indicated above.

»The continual observation and superintendence, the absence of all that can do harm, in the mode of life and occupations, are essential points in a curative proceeding which has for its object gradually to strengthen the enfeebled muscles, to restore the reduced or suppressed functions of the articulations, as well as to remove existing disorders in the circulation (thromboses, swellings, hardnesses &c.).

»The personal acquaintance with each patient which extends even to a knowledge of the state of each of his muscles and articulations, makes it possible to determine the measure of his general capacity at the same time that it protects the patient from over-exertion and leads to complete voluntary activity. Owing to this process of individualisation with its scrupulous control, *dissemblers* and *exaggerators* do not long succeed in deceiving the physician as to the real state of their ability to work.

»The gymnastic treatment which stimulates appetite and assimilation is combined with substantial feeding corresponding to the ordinary diet at the hospitals of our city ($\frac{1}{2}$ lb. of meat, 1 lb. of bread, 2 milk rolls, greens and potatoes, coffee twice, soup once, and two bottles of ale.) Weighings taken weekly, prove increase of weight in almost all the patients (in some cases 10, 12 or 18 lbs); the weight has remained the same in a small minority; in 3 patients (out of 125) it has diminished 2 lbs., and finally, in one, 4 lbs.

»As a whole the arrangements have proved good and suitable for their object. In all the cases where this was possible, constant progress in the recovery has been noted. Though it has sometimes happened that patients have opposed a certain indifference and even more or less open resistance to our efforts, they have generally shown confidence in the treatment and supported it with good will and intelligence. Many expressions of gratitude, when leaving the Home, for the treatment, often painful enough, also prove that the joy of recovering the use of their limbs makes them forget the loss of the indemnification.

»The administrators and the physicians of the establishment have been supported and encouraged in their work by numerous proofs of confidence and flattering appreciation on the part of the medical body. The consciousness of co-operation in an important work so rich in blessings, has helped us to support patiently the attacks of ridicule and envy. Our best reward has been the success attained, the ever growing confidence the young establishment enjoys and will always try to retain among corporations, arbitrators, and other authorities.

Frequentation of the Home.

From Jan. 2nd to May 31st 1891:

Entered . . . . 131 patients
Discharged . . . . 82 »

Still under treatment June 4:th . . . . 49 »

»Relatively to the different parts of the body the lesions are divided in the following manner:

1. *Fractures.*
   a. simple, i. e. without lesion of soft parts . 47
   b. complex, i. e. with lesion of soft parts . . 19
2. *Contusions* 5
3. *Lesions of soft parts* 5
4. *Luxations* (all in the shoulder joint) 4
5. *Sprains and dislocations* 2

, »In serious cases the treatment of the first consequences of the accident has almost invariably taken place at the hospitals where the injured have generally been received on the day of the accident.

»As regards the solution of the second part of the medical work, the removal of the *indirect consequences* of the accident, which present themselves only in the course of the primary treatment or remain after the healing of the injured limb, and the persistance of which is often the single cause of the diminution or cessation of ability to work, experience has shown that scarcely half the number of patients have found suitable and continued medical treatment on leaving the hospital. Most frequently, months have passed unemployed, and unfortunately the most important time for helping functional disorders, as well as for removing morbid alterations due to forced inactivity or unsuitable use of the injured limb, is neglected. Anchylosis of bones and articulations, atrophy of ligaments, capsules and muscles, and partial paralysis: such have been the consequences of injuries which might have been cured by consistent and timely use of mechanical gymnastics. To what has been said before, we will add that the time for beginning the treatment has been relatively late. *With our 82 patients discharged, there have been on an average 12 or 13 months between the accident and entrance to the Home.* The period of entrance has varied between the 3rd and 63rd month after the accident.

»The length of treatment at the Home has been from 2 to 128 days for the patients discharged up to this date. It gives an average time of 53,1 days or about 7 $1/2$ weeks. Several of the patients asked for dismissal as soon as they were more or less capable of some light kind of work. Sometimes their departure has been premature, notwithstanding the advice and insistance of the physician that they should remain. The ruinous state of pecuniary circumstances, principally of married men, long incapable of work, and which the indemnification has been powerless to prevent, was in some cases the decisive cause for leaving, and often we have had much trouble to hinder an interruption of treatment as injurious to the patient as to the corporation to which he belonged.

»The tables of Dr. G. SCHÜTZ[1] give particulars as to the results of treatment. They also show the estimated ability to work before and after the treatment.

»Of 80 patients discharged (2 are out of the account as the exact figures regarding them are missing) 10 recovered *full ability to work*, 17 remained, temporarily, slightly incapacitated for work, (up to $1/4$ of the incapacity), and were discharged with continued precautionary indemnification (»*Schonungsrente*»).

»Important improvements have been obtained in 32 cases and it has been possible to raise the ability to work:

in 2 cases by 100 %
»   2   »   »   80   »
»   1   »   »   70   »
»   4   »   » $66^2/_3$ »
»   8   »   »   60   »
»   1   »   »   55   »
»   9   »   »   50   ».

---

[1] Unfortunately we are obliged to omit this table for want of room. Therefore we refer persons who may be interested in the matter to G. SCHÜTZ: Erster Jahresbericht, 1891, über die Thätigkeit der Heimstätte für V.ıeletzte zu Nieder-Schönhausen bei Berlin.

»In 15 other cases the increase of ability to work has been from 25 % to 45 %.

»In 14 cases it has been raised from 10 % to 20 %.

» 5 » » » » » to 10 % or a little less.

» 8 » the result has been 0 % or at least not considerable enough to infer any increase.

»Including the 8 cases in which the result was nil or nearly so, the *increase of ability to work* on *an average* amounted to *37,6 %*.

»If we consider the sum of money represented by this percentage of the general improvement, a sum which the Associations would have had to pay perhaps during 20 or 30 years, we are justified in saying that the results are brilliant, and they will be still more so, when the patients can be moved directly to the Home from the Hospital.

»It is also quite evident that only the Zander gymnastic apparatus alone make the treatment of the patients possible on so large a scale and at so moderate a price. A treatment of the kind would be quite impossible with nothing but hands at one's disposal. To the decidedly higher price of the manual treatment would be added the difficulty of finding, for such fatiguing and troublesome work, a sufficient number of practically and theoretically instructed assistants.»

In the towns of Bochum (Westphalia), Königshütte (Silesia) and Neu-Rahnsdorf near Berlin Convalescent Homes, on the pattern of the one at Nieder-Schönhausen, have been founded, and, moreover, workmen dis-abled by accidents are treated at almost all the medico-mechanical Zander Institutes of Germany.

IX.

The treatment of scoliosis.

By degress we have passed through the vast domain in which the importance of gymnastic treatment for numerous morbid forms is most clearly evident. We ardently wishthat nobody may see, in these successive descriptions, the expression of excessive enthusiasm only, but rather the conviction of an unprejudiced critic, desiring to make proselytes to his doctrines confirmed by experience, amongst more or less sceptical colleagues. Within the domain of science there exist few classes so conservative as that of medical men. They frequently adhere to the authority of their own studies and to the results obtained by them, with such remarkable tenacity, that irresistible arguments and reasons of special weight are required to shake their conservatism and to make way for new ideas and views hitherto outside their range of studies.

If we have succeeded in throwing some rays of light on a sphere which has not been either sufficiently known or appreciated, our efforts have not been vain. But we have also to appeal to the indulgence of the reader for the sincere and undisguised expression of our convictions. That is what we do also on approaching the key-stone of our work, the treatment of one of the morbid forms in which gymnastics with their true ally and assistant, orthopedy, should really be considered as a specific. This disease, its ætiology and the history of its various treatments could easily furnish material for as many pages as this present work contains. We mean the pathological or morbid change of the spine and its muscles, which is called *scoliosis*. If this affection did not exist, the number of female patients at our Institutes would be very limited. But what woman is inclined to keep all her life an infirmity which, in some cases imperceptible, in others often takes such threatening dimensions as to poison the existence of the young woman. Really, the number of scoliotic affections is predominant in woman-kind to such a degree, and the disease and its symptoms are of such importance in woman that scoliosis may rightly be termed a *woman's disease*.

In medical practice there have never been constructed so many hypotheses or tried so many methods of treatment as for this disease. While some see its origin in morbid changes of the muscles, it is but natural that they should exclusively direct the treatment on the latter, and employ gymnastics. According to others, the cause of scoliosis is, on the contrary, much deeper, in so much as it affects the vertebræ as well as the ligaments, and that we must see in it a constitutional anomaly which can be traced to the embryonic state. For them, orthopedic treatment is all: extension-beds and bandages of all possible and impossible shapes, so that there is scarcely one orthopedist or maker of surgical instruments who has not invented a new kind of bandage. We think Dr. NEBEL gives a correct opinion in quoting the Swedish physician and orthopedist, HERMAN SÄTHERBERG, who said, 40 years ago, that the truth is only arrived at by a combination of gymnastic and bandage-treatment. »When medical gymnastics», continues NEBEL, »pretend to be the only rational remedy for curvatures of the spine, they much overshoot the mark; but they would on the contrary, be fully justified in taking the *first* rank among the remedies employed for that disease.

»In Sweden, notwithstanding the praiseworthy efforts tending to give children a better carriage by making them employ their own agents, the muscles, it is often overlooked that we have before us symptoms compelling us to counteract threatening changes in the ligamentous apparatus and the skeleton. In Germany it is too frequently forgotten that, in contending against deformities resulting from the unequal pressure on the vertebræ in unsymmetrical carriage of the body, the bandages used are but a feeble remedy to the local affection, and that the general health is much endangered, if one does not work simultaneously, by gymnastics, on the maintenance of the mobility of the articulations of the vertebræ and on the exercise of muscles which become atrophied by inaction. For slight and simple scolioses corsets and other apparatus are frequently used in cases where gymnastic treatment would be the only proper remedy, and unfortunately many physicians consider they have done enough by prescribing a corset. Often the correction effected by the corset is only very slight in proportion to the injury done to mobility, to health and strength by keeping back and chest immovable, and by neglecting a suitable general treatment.

»If gymnastics are unable to remove, permanently, the unequal pressure on the deformed vertebræ, and if they often cannot cure, they will nevertheless enable the more or less scoliotic patient, to hold himself better, and to a certain degree he will continue to do so, thus to some extent counteracting increasing deformity. The victim of an exclusive bandage-treat-

ment will remain crippled, with stiffened, weak limbs, totally
dependent on his expensive apparatus, which often requires repa-
ration and renewal.» Dr. NEBEL has in the above lines perfectly
characterised the two existing schools with their advantages and
their weak points.

We have not yet gained full clearness as to the essence of
this disease. A very important contribution to the knowledge
of its pathological anatomy and of its pathogeny has, however,
been furnished by Professor A. LORENZ of Vienna in his work:
»Die Pathologie und Theraphie der seitlichen Rückgratsverkrüm-
mungen.» Vienna 1866. A means which has also made an epoch
in the more profound knowledge of scoliosis and its mechanical
disproportion has been given us in the two trunk-measuring-
apparatus constructed by Dr. ZANDER, one in the year 1882
and the other in 1887. »At first», says ZANDER in the Nord.
Med. Arkiv (Scandinavian Medical Records) Vol. XXI, N:o 22,
»the treatment of this morbid affection was of no particular interest to me, for I lacked what I considered an indispensable
condition for a really scientific proceeding, namely, an instrument
which allowed of my easily determining the carriage and form
of the body. How could it otherwise be possible to obtain
a sure diagnosis and a sufficiently exact appreciation of the
effect of different movements and of the general results of the
treatment?»

In another work we have expressed our opinion on the
measuring-apparatus in these words: »All the works of man are
liable to defects, for the human hand does not produce anything
perfectly faultless, but in our opinion ZANDER's apparatus approaches the ideal of perfection. When there appear no errors
of measurement as regards the character of the scoliosis, one
cannot but have confidence in the apparatus, and by what other
instruments can this measuring be more exactly made? It is
true that to a superficial observer the figures obtained offer
inexplicable peculiarities and even slight errors, but, if the
measuring is repeated at short intervals and the ·figures compared, these errors will soon be discovered and their causes explained. One of the great advantages of the diagram obtained by the measuring is, that we can follow the degrees of
the effect of the treatment and we are immediately able to judge

if and to what extent we have *overcorrected* the curvature. This
control has frequently had brilliant results. »The price of an
apparatus of the kind», says ZANDER, »is unfortunately somewhat
high. But as it is an apparatus for measuring on a large
scale, and the manufacturing of which requires the greatest
exactness in every detail, and which cannot be produced *en
gros*, it cannot be supplied at a more moderate price. However,
even this price ought not to be considered in a question of treating in the course of every year some fifty patients or more,
afflicted with scoliosis.»

Any one who has read the works published during the last
years on this disease, will have no difficulty in understanding
that there exist, as causes of the evil, infinitely deeper changes
than hypertrophied muscles on one side and atrophied muscles
on the other, and that efforts exclusively destined to develop the
muscles are incapable of leading to the cure of scoliosis. Also,
by the construction of his apparatus, ZANDER has caused an immense step to be taken in the treatment of this disease. Even if we
recognise his ideas in some of his predecessors, yet we consider
ZANDER as the one who has made the way, since he has succeeded in solving the question in a much more simple, a less
violent, but still a decisive manner. In his work on the treatment of habitual scoliosis by means of mechanical gymnastics,
he shows with the utmost clearness that habitual bad carriage
is frequently the basis on which the disease is developed in increasingly grave forms.

»Professor LORENZ of Vienna», says Dr. Zander, »gives us the
following definition of habitual scoliosis: »The scoliotic carriage,
permanently fixed by the alteration of ligaments and skeleton.»
If this definition were perfectly just, the activity of orthopedists
with regard to scoliosis would be very limited and have scarcely
any chance of success. I think one had better say: »A scoliotic
carriage more or less fixed», and, in other places, Dr. LORENZ
shows that this is really what he means. In fact, why should
we not designate those lateral curvatures of the spine as scoliosis, wich the patient himself is able to correct fully or partially, certainly with effort and sometimes only for a short
space of time? In both cases, however, there is a determined
pathological state, for the suppression of which are required

therapeutic measures often demanding great efforts. From being physiological, the scoliotic carriage becomes pathological, and it passes to the latter form by habit, in as much as the patient assumes this attitude as soon as he is off his guard. Then we can be perfectly certain that there have appeared unsymmetrical alterations in the constituent parts of the spine. If under the name of scoliosis we understand all such lateral curvatures which really are an object for the efforts of the orthopedist, we should say: »Habitual scoliosis is a scoliotic carriage which has passed into an habitual state». But where is the cause of scoliotic carriage? The cause is to be found, I think, in the too sedentary life of the young, due in its turn to the exaggerated claims of school-education. It is not my task to examine here whether these claims are legitimate, and from what point of view they are so. But, in the capacity of medical gymnast and physician, having had to treat yearly hundreds of young girls, weak and overworked, I have been able to note perfectly the consequences of the existing disproportion between the amount of work required and the amount that can be done without peril to the physical development.

»Why have we not girls' schools in which the intellectual development, belonging certainly to more mature years, leaves more time for the work of physical development? The precious years of growth, have they not the high mission of forming a healthy, vigorous and hardy body? If this mission obtained due attentention instead of being carelessly put aside, a check would be imposed on the painful disease which now occupies us, a disease easily guarded against in its mildest form, but which, having once attained a certain degree, resists all the efforts of art and science.

»As we have just said, the scoliotic carriage begins by being physiological i. e. that the spine makes the flexions and torsions compatible with its normal structure. These deviations from a straight carriage are a consequence of the fact that the active agents, the muscles, become tired and relaxed, especially in consequence of the great amount of writing to be done at school and at home. Then there is the ordinary disproportion between the height of the seat and that of the desk and the insufficient size of the latter which literally compels the pupil to lean on

one side, generally to the left, in order to give more place to
the right arm. When the physiological limits of the movement
of the articulations are reached, and the muscles operating as
active ligaments become inactive, it is no longer the supporting
elements of the spine, the vertebræ, which alone carry the weight
of the body, but also the ligamentous and bony parts which prevent the extension of the movement beyond physiological limits.
The weight of the body is, as it were, suspended on these arresting parts. And, as it happens daily and for several hours
during all the years of school-life, it is not surprising if these
parts which are not made for that purpose, gradually give way,
become weak, deformed and disproportionately extended. Let
us add that the pressure on the vertebræ in a case of scoliosis,
is gradually conveyed to the concave part, in proportion as the
vertebræ deviate from the line of gravity of the body, resulting
in the wedge-shaped deformity of the vertebræ. Besides even
insignificant alterations in the constituent parts of the spine in-
jure the whole mechanism, causing difficulties or obstacles in
the work of the muscles (which is to straighten the spine) and
confusing the patient's own consciousness of the correct
carriage.

»Therefore, when the scoliosis has attained a certain degree
of development, it has an ever increasing tendency to develop
further. Abandoned to itself, it frequently increases with fright-
ful rapidity, and we have to be thankful if, when it is at last
subjected to treatment, its further development is arrested. Even
cases, offering a chance of improvement, put the skill and therapeutic means of the orthopedist to a severe test, especially
when, as is generally the case, 7 or 8 hours of work at school
and at home pull down what the treatment may have built up
in one hour.

»Can gymnastic treatment have any chance of success at
all in such an unequal fight? Unhesitatingly I answer this question in the affirmative, for results have been obtained even in
cases where I was doubtful myself; results such that, according
to my opinion, there would be no more cases of grave habitual
scoliosis, if sufficient time, in proportion to the difficulties to
be overcome, were given to the treatment, and if the affection
were not entrusted too late to the medical gymnast.

»It would not therefore be necessary that the whole time of treatment should be longer; on the contrary, if it were more concentrated in the beginning, and applied with more energy, it would give greater results in an infinitely shorter time, and later there would be required only a preservative treatment, occupying much less time and more calculated to strengthen the body in general. This latter treatment, one hour of gymnastics every day, would, however, be indispensable, considering that the causes of scoliosis extend their influence over the entire school-period, and that it is necessary to be ever on one's guard against eventual relapses. A thorough treatment, such as I imagine it, can but be put into practice, however, by the establishment of orthopedic Institutes where the patients would at the same time be boarders, where all would tend to the aim of subjecting them the whole day to corrective influences, where the studies would not indeed be neglected, but so arranged as not to put obstacles in the way of the principal purpose of the establishment. I am fully convinced that six months passed at an establishment of that kind would be more effective than two years of ordinary treatment: in winter one hour a day, in summer, perhaps no treatment at all. But such an undertaking will never be realized without vigorous support on the part of physicians.

«And, to return to the treatment at my Institute, the leading principle is to make corrective influences, as continued and as vigorous as possible, act on the patients during the hour of gymnastics. The unsymmetrical modifications which soon appear and continually increase in the spine must be energetically suppressed. It is as if all these alterations formed an inclined plane on which the weight of the body presses incessantly, giving ever increasing dimensions to the spinal curvature. Our efforts therefore tend to make the weight of the body act on the opposite side, so that the various effects of the pressure appear on the less compressed half of the vertebræ and intervertebral cartilages. In this manner a flexibility, equal on both sides of the spine, will be restored and the tendency to lean always to one and the same side will be considerably diminished. This *static* part of the treatment, during which the patient remains completely passive, can be accomplished in various ways.

98

But the muscles must co-operate. We know to what changes tone and elasticity are submitted, when the points of insertion of the muscles are brought nearer or farther from each other for any length of time. If we sit with our backs crooked for some time, we cannot straighten ourselves up as easily as immediately after assuming the bent attitude, and this difficulty becomes greater the weaker the muscles are. As long as the curvature of the spine is stiff and fixed, the muscles naturally can contribute very little to its straightening; but as soon as a certain flexibility is noticeable, the muscles have to do the important work of straightening the curvatures as much as possible, and thus contribute to the distribution of normal pressure on the deformed vertebræ. The static treatment should be combined with the dynamic treatment, for they mutually complete each other, and they do not form a whole until the moment they act in common. This rule has also always been observed at the Gymnastic Orthopedic Institute of Stockholm.»

The study of these diseases is so complicated, and presupposes such profound knowledge as well in anatomy as in mechanics, that we are justified in doubting that our ordinary Swedish gymnasts (we do not mean here our medical gymnasts) understand the disease in all its extension, and even that they are able to judge it rightly. In the following serious words Dr. ZANDER protests against the treatment of scoliosis by incompetent persons: »It would be unjust to require that young gymnasts, alone, without the necessary knowledge for an exact objective comprehension of the pathological case confided to them and without special apparatus, should be able to effect what will perhaps be possible only at an Orthopedic Institute with its greater resources, from the point of view of the diagnosis as well as of treatment and control. That the gymnasts nevertheless take upon themselves this task, shows most clearly that they have no idea of the difficulties combined with the treatment of scoliosis. Or, can the exceedingly complicated problem of correcting a curved spine be left with less hesitation than in other kinds of work, to persons without the necessary skill? Would a chiefly mechanical work, under other circumstances, be entrusted to a person who neither has shown any taste for mechanics, nor possesses the preliminary knowledge requisite for mecha-

nical problems? Though occupied all my life with the employment of mechanics in the service of medecine, a lengthy medi-
tation is often necessary to enable me to so compose a movement
that it has the effect I want and no other. Besides, scoliosis
cannot be treated by one person alone, without instructed assistants, and apparatus specially constructed *ad hoc*. In the most
favorable cases such treatment is only loss of time, but usually
it becomes fatal by the neglect of precious time in which something might really have been done against the evil.»

Certain gymnasts maintain that slight degrees of scoliosis can
be cured by pedagogic gymnastics, i. e. by strengthening bilateral
movements, but that is a mistake, for the development of the
muscles is one thing, and the correction of the pathological carriage
another (see ZANDER 1. c. page 20). This statement does not in
any way diminish the importance of pedagogic gymnastics as
an exellent prophylactic, perfectly appreciated in Sweden. There
often occur relapses in the disease during the years of growth,
for the causes which produce it continue to exist, and therefore
a constant treatment during the whole school-period of the young
girl is essential for ensuring the arrest or the cure of the disease.
A bandage, however ingeniously it may be constructed, can certainly contribute to sustain the body and correct the curvature,
but without simultaneous use of gymnastics it cannot arrest or
remove the evil, and, employed alone, it is, if I am permitted
to say so, worse than useless, for it frequently happens that
under the corset the scoliosis assumes grave forms of development.

The results that ZANDER has obtained by his treatment, are
stated in the tables of Dr. NEBEL in his work (pp. 351—353).
The report of diagrammatic measurings will also be found
there, as well as in Dr. HASEBROEK's work.

X.

Means of treatment of scoliosis.

The *number of apparatus* necessary at an Institute established in a small provincial town, or at a bathing-place, is neither so large nor so expensive that the purchase of them can cause any difficulties. In fact, according to Zander's opinion the following apparatus will in most cases be sufficient:

K 1, K 2, K 3, K 4, K 5, L 1, L 2, L 3, L 4, L 5, L 6, A 2, A 3, C 1, C 5, C 6, C 7, C 8, C 10, and *last but not least* the trunkmeasuring-apparatus. The apparatus for cross-cut-measuring is no doubt most interesting and useful, but it is not absolutely necessary.

In the following pages we will, after ZANDER, indicate the principles and the object of the apparatus mentioned, beginning by those most characteristically orthopedic.

The object of these apparatus is to exercise a corrective influence by means of suitable pressure applied on the abnormal curvatures of the spine. By these corrections we cause, on one side, the tension of the contracted muscles and ligaments which fix the vertebræ in an oblique or contorted position to each other, and on the other side we *cause* the diminution of pressure on the part of the intervertebral disc situated in the concavity of the curvature, while the part situated in the convexity is subjected to stronger pressure. This effect is facilitated or increased if the patient occupies a reclining or suspended position which diminishes the pressure of the weight of the body on the spine, and even causes the tension of the latter by one part of the weight of the body.

FIRST GROUP.

K 1.

Lateral suspension (reclining).

The apparatus exercises corrective influence upon lateral curvature in total C-shaped, or upon dorsal curvature in S-shaped scoliosis.

K 2.

Lateral pressure (lying).

The apparatus serves to exercise a corrective action on lumbar curvatures.

K 3.

Chest-rotation.

The object of this apparatus is to counteract, diminish or remove that most dangerous, and most difficult to overcome of all the symptoms of scoliosis: the rotation of the vertebræ and distorsion of the thorax. It is most frequently made use of in dorsal curvatures, but it is also employed with advantage in lumbar curvatures, even without rotation. It is easy to ascertain the powerful and appropriate effect on the thorax by considering the change of shape of the thorax under its influence.

It is natural that it cannot alone produce real improvement in the shape of the thorax unless combined with active gymnastic movements, which correct the torsion, straighten the curvatures and expand the thorax. Much patience and a consistent use of the apparatus, according to the age of the patient and the development of the scoliosis, are indispensable for it is an indisputable truth, that it is impossible to *make* a spinal curvature straight, but possible to compel it to *grow* straight.

K 4.

Redressing of lumbar scoliosis (sitting).

The apparatus is chiefly designed for correcting lumbar curvatures or total curvatures of the spinal column, so as to bend the spine as possible in the opposite direction.

•

K 5.

Lateral pressure (sitting).

The object of this apparatus is to reduce, by pressure on the convexity of the curvature, the unilateral pressure on the dorsal vertebræ, or remove it to the opposite side. The patient simultaneously makes certain arm-movements causing the unilateral or bilateral contraction of the dorsal muscles.

SECOND GROUP.

The apparatus of the second group i. e. the apparatus for orthopedic exercises, act on abnormal curvatures of the spine, not only actively by exercising the muscles that influence the carriage of the spinal column, but also by arrangements passively correcting the abnormal carriage and curvatures.

L 1.

Combination of A 3 and D 1.

This apparatus has for object a simultaneous effect on the dorsal and the lumbar curvatures; on the dorsal curvature by passive tension of one of the arms with or without active sinking of the other, or by active sinking of both arms; on the lumbar curvature by the lateral inclination of the seat. These two movements can be combined in different manners for acting on single or double curvatures.

L 2.

Strengthening of the lumbar region (lying).

The object of this apparatus is to strengthen the dorsal muscles in general, or principally those of one side. In both

cases, the trunk is in a suspended horizontal position for the
purpose, either of dividing the efforts between both sides, or,
when only one side of the muscles is acted on, to exercise
stronger pressure upon those halves of the vertebræ which are
in the convexity of the curvature. The exercises are made while
the patient is lying face down, or on one side. The patient
whose legs are kept down by a special contrivance, raises the
upper part of the trunk and keeps it for a few moments in a
horizontal or a curved position. The first-named movement is
vigorous, but by no means violent; it brings into more or less
activity all the dorsal muscles. The latter movement is almost
exclusively employed in unilateral curvatures of the spine and
while taking it, the patient leans on the side against which
the concavity is turned.

L 3.

Carrying the pelvis sideways.

In lateral curvatures of the spine the patients often have a
tendency to displace the upper part of their trunk to one side
or the other. The apparatus has for object to exercise the patient in carrying the inferior part of the trunk towards the same
side and thus to restore the correct vertical position. In this
apparatus therefore, the upper part of the trunk is fixed, while
the lower part is moved and has to overcome a greater or smaller
resistance. This displacement at the same time causes the correction of the curvature of the spine.

L 4.

Carrying the pelvis forwards, backwards.

The special purpose of this apparatus is to counteract or
diminish lumbar lordosis and flat back, and sometimes also to
remedy a too great or too slight inclination of the pelvis. In
the first case the abdominal and gluteal muscles are chiefly
acted on; in the second the sacrolumbar muscles and the
iliopsoas.

L 5.

Lateral flexion of the lumbar spine.

Flexion of the lumbar part of the back and of the whole back to the side opposite to the curvature, while the arms and the thorax are fixed. It is most essential that the fixation should be done correctly according as single or double curvature has to be treated.

L 6.

Straightening of the spine.

In a sitting posture the patient straightens and stretches his spine to the utmost possible, and, meanwhile raises with his head a lever with a movable weight. This movement cannot be made until a certain suppleness of the dorsal curvatures has been attained, but it is then of great utility.

A 2.

Arm-raising.

The object of this movement is to act, in the treatment of scoliosis, on the spinal curvature and on the carriage of the shoulder. The movement in question acts partly on the deltoid muscle, partly on those that extend from the neck and spine, as well as from the sides of the thorax to the shoulder-blade, and finally on the extensor muscles of the arm. It is a powerful inspiratory-movement which causes the expansion of the thorax.

C 5.

Trunk-extension (standing).

The object of this movement is to strengthen the back-muscles in general (this movement is gentler than L 2) while acting on the lumbar curvature by the patient's resting the foot of the convex side on a board of heights varying as occasion requires. This apparatus acts on a great number of muscles of the back of the body, from the neck to the calves.

C 6.

Trunk-sideways-flexion.

This movement acts on the dorsal and abdominal muscles on the side which performs the movement, as well as on the elevator muscles of one of the shoulders and on the depressors of the other. The curvature is straightened, and the spine bent over on the other side, if sufficient mobility exists.

C 7.

Trunk-rotation.

This movement causes the rotation of the upper part of the trunk, while the pelvis is fixed. It acts as well on the abdominal as on the dorsal muscles.

C 8.

Pelvis-turning.

This movement, on the contrary, acts on the inferior part of the trunk, while the superior part is fixed, and exercises its principal effect on the lumbar region of the spine. If the upper part of an elastic rod is twisted like the spine, while the lower part is fixed, the angle of torsion will naturally reach its maximum at the upper end and according as each part approaches the fixed end, the torsion will be less. It follows that in the apparatus C 7 it is the upper part of the spine which is subjected to the greatest torsion, while in the apparatus C 8 the torsion is strongest in the lower part of the spine, since then the upper part is fixed. This torsion, however, is chiefly accomplished in the dorsal vertebræ, as the power of rotation is excessively small in the lumbar vertebræ.

C 10.

Neck-extension.

This movement acts as well on the extensors of the neck as on the flexors of the head.

With the knowledge of a correct application of all these apparatus, and of the modifications of which they are capable, one is sufficiently armed for the struggle against the affection called scoliosis.

Literature.

Aall, Dr. L., Bylæge. Den mekaniske Gymnastik. Kristiania 1885, Grøndahl & Sön.

Aktiebolaget Göransson's Mekaniska Verkstad. Kurzgefasste Uebersicht über Dr. G. Zander's Medico-Mechanische Gymnastikmethode von Dr. A. Levertin, und einige Anweisungen bezüglich der Anlage gymnastischer Institute nach jener Methode, von Der Aktien-Gesellschaft Göranssons Mekaniska Verkstad. Stockholm 1892.

— — Exposé succinct de la Gymnastique Médico-Mécanique Zander par Le Dr. A. Levertin, et quelques indications sur la création d'établissements gymnastique d'après cette méthode par La société anonyme Göransson's Mekaniska Verkstad. Stockholm 1892.

— — A short review of Dr. G. Zander's Medico-Mechanical Gymnastic Method by Dr. A. Levertin, and some directions for the establishment of gymnastic institutes on this method by The Göranssons Mekaniska Verkstad Company Limited. Stockholm 1893.

Bähr, Dr. F. Prospekt No. 2 für die Unfall-Berufsgenossenschaften des Deutschen Reichs. Medico-mechanisches Institut Karlsruhe. 1891.

— — Die Zander'sche Behandlung der Skoliosen. Zeitschrift für Orthopädische Chirurgie. II Band. 3 Heft. Stuttgart 1892.

Bernacchi, Dr. L. Gli Apparecchi per la Cura Ginnastica Medicomeccanica ed il modo d'adoperarli. Milano 1881.

— — La Cura della Scoliosi cogli Apparecchi del Dott. G. Zander, Archivio di Ortopedia. Anno VIII, Milano, 1891.

Bertling, Dr. A. Die Zander'sche medico-mechanische Behandlungs-Methode, ihre Definition und Indicationen. Prospect aus der Aachener Medico-mechanischen Zander-Anstalt. Köln 1893.

Friedmann, Dr. M. und Heuck, Dr. G. Erster Jahresbericht über die Wirksamkeit des Gymnastisch-Orthopädischen Instituts in Mannheim 1889.

Hasebroek, Dr. K. Das Hamburger Medico-mechanische Institut nebst Bericht über dessen Wirksamkeit im Jahre 1889. Hamburg.

— — Die Erschütterungen in der Zander'schen Heilgymnastik in physiologischer und therapeutischer Beziehung. Hamburg 1890. Otto Meissner.

— — Mittheilungen aus dem Hamburger Medico-mechanischen Institut vom Jahre 1890. Hamburg, 1891. Otto Meissner.

— — Ueber die Nervosität und den Mangel an körperlicher Bewegung in der Gross-stadt (Ein Beitrag zur hygieinischen Bedeutung der Medico-mechanischen Institute). Hamburg 1891. Otto Meissner.

— — Mittheilungen aus dem Hamburger Medico-mechanischen Institut vom Jahre 1891. Hamburg 1892.

— — Die Mechanische Heilgymnastik des Dr. Gustaf Zander und die Medico-mechanischen Institute, Vortrag im Verein für öffentliche Gesundheitspflege in Hamburg. Hamburg 1892. Johannes Kriebel.

— — Ueber die Nachbehandlung Verletzter im Hamburger Medicomechan. Institut. Hamburg 1893. Otto Meissner.

Heiligenthal, Dr. F. Die Apparate für Mechanische Heilgymnastik und deren Anwendung im Grossherzogl. Friedrichsbade in Baden-Baden. 1886.

— — Ueber das Friedrichsbad. Aerztliche Mittheilungen aus Baden. Jahrg. XLII N:r 5. Karlsruhe 1888.

— — Mittheilungen aus dem Grossherzoglichen Friedrichsbade in Baden-Baden vom Sommer 1888. Karlsruhe 1889.

Hönig, Dr. Ueber Simulation und Uebertreibung der Unfallverletzten und deren Bekämpfung nebst einer Statistik über die im Breslauer Medico-mechanischen Institute behandelten Verletzten. Breslau 1891.

Hunt, Dr. W. The Mechanico-therapeutic & Zander Institute in Baden-Baden. Philadelphia 1890.

Krüche, Dr. A. Die Schwedische Bewegungskur. Ein Heilmittel vieler chronischer Leiden. Berlin 1891. Hugo Steinitz.

Kühner, Dr. A. Dr. G. Zander's mechanische Behandlungsmethode in ihrer Bedeutung für Gesunde und Kranke. »Gesundheit», Zeitschrift für öffentliche und private Hygieine. Jahrg. XVI N:r 9, 11, 14, 17, 20. Frankfurt a. M. 1891.

— — Dr. G. Zanders' mechanische Behandlungsmethode in ihrer Bedeutung für Gesunde und Kranke. »Blätter für Klinische Hydrotherapie». Jahrg. I. N:r 7. Wien 1891.

Levertin, Dr. A. Begagnas sjukgymnastiken i den utsträckning den förtjänar? (Are medico-mechanical gymnastics used in proportion to their value?) Stockholm 1891.

— — Dr. G. Zander's Medico-Mechanische Gymnastik, Ihre Methode, Bedeutung und Anwendung, nebst Auszügen aus der einschlägigen Litteratur. Illustrated edition. Stockholm 1892.

— — La Gymnastique Médico-Mécanique Zander, — Méthode, Importance, Application. Illustrated edition. Stockholm 1893.

Lövinson, Dr. E. Mittheilungen aus dem Berliner Medico-mechanischen Institut. Erstes Heft. Bemerkungen über Habituelle Scoliose. Berlin 1893. F. Schneider & Co.

Mazzucchelli, Dr. L. La Ginnastica Medica, cogli apparecchi meccanici del dott. Zander. Milano 1888.

Nebel, Dr. H. Ueber Heilgymnastik und Massage. Volkmanns Sammlung klinischer Vorträge N:r 286. Leipzig 1886.

— — Referat über Hünerfauths »Geschichte der Massage». Deutsche Med. Wochenschrift N:o 6, Leipzig 1887.

— — Betrachtung über Scoliose im Anschluss an Besprechung der Lorenz'schen Monographie. Deutsche Med. Wochenschrift N:r 26—31, Leipzig 1887.

— — Briefe aus Schweden. Deutsche Med. Wochenschrift N:r 41—44, Leipzig 1887.

— — »Terrain- und Bergsteigeapparate». Deutsche Med. Wochenschrift N:o 50. Leipzig 1888.

— — Beiträge zur Mechanischen Behandlung, mit besonderer Berücksichtigung der schwedischen Heilgymnastik speciell der mechanischen Gymnastik des Dr. Gust. Zander. Wiesbaden 1888. J. F. Bergmann.

— — Behandlung des Muskelrheumatismus. Deutsche Med. Wochenschrift N:r 32, Leipzig 1889.

— — Einiges über die Würdigung der schwedischen Heilgymnastik in der deutschen «Massage»-Litteratur. Schmidts Jahrbücher. Band CCXXX p. 193.

Nebel, Dr. H. Einige Bemerkungen über die 3. Auflage des Dr. J. Schreiber'schen Werkes über Massage. Deutsche med. Wochenschrift 1889.

— — Bewegungskuren mittelst schwedischer Heilgymnastik und Massage mit besonderer Berücksichtigung der mechanischen Behandlung des Dr. G. Zander. Wiesbaden 1889. J. F. Bergmann.

— — Die Behandlung mittelst Bewegungen und Massage. Wiesbaden 1891. J. F. Bergmann.

— — Mittheilungen über die Zander'sche Mechanotherapie, Separatabdruck aus »Zeitschrift für orthopädische Chirurgie». II Band 1893.

Ramdohr, Dr. H. Ueber die maschinelle Heilgymnastik Dr. Zander's etc. Extrait de Schmidt's Jahrbücher Band CCXVII.

— — Die Heilgymnastik, gemeinverständlich dargestellt. Illustrated edition. Leipzig 1893. J. J. Weber.

Roth, Dr. M. Prospect aus der Mechano-therapeutischen Ordinations-Anstalt. Wien 1889.

— — Mittheilungen der Wiener Mechano-therapeutischen Anstalt. Das Zander'sche Heilverfahren. Illustrated edition. Wien 1892.

Schütz, Dr. G. Medico-Mechanische Institute. Zweck und Bedeutung für die Berufsgenossenschaften. »Der Kompass», Organ der Knappschafts-Berufsgenossenschaft für das deutsche Reich, Jahrg. V N:r 10, Berlin 1890.

— — Aerztlicher Bericht über die Thätigkeit der Heimstätte für Verletzte zu Nieder-Schönhausen bei Berlin 1891.

— — Erster Jahresbericht 1891 über die Thätigkeit der Heimstätte für Verletzte zu Nieder-Schönhausen bei Berlin. 1892. F. Schneider & Co.

Wischnewetzky, Dr. L. Contributions to Mechanico-Therapeutics and Orthopedics:

Vol. 1, No. 1. The Mechanico-Therapeutic Institute by Dr. Gustaf Zander. — New York 1891.

Vol. 1, No. 2. Mechanico-Therapeutics and Orthopedics by means of Apparatus by Dr. Gustaf Zander. — New York 1891.

Vol. 1, No. 3. The Mechanical Treatment of Chorea. A. Historico-critical study by Dr. Hermann Nebel. New York 1891.

Wretlind, Dr. E. W. Om rörelsekuren eller Kinesitherapien (On Kinesipathy), Gothenburg 1884. N. J. Gumpert.

Zander, Dr. G. Medico-Mekaniska Institutet i Stockholm 1871.

— — Om Mediko-Mekaniska Institutet i Stockholm (On the medico-mechanical Institute of Stockholm). Nord. Med. Archiv, Band IV N:r 9, 1872.

— — The Mechanico-therapeutic Institution in Stockholm, established in 1865. Philadelphia 1876.

— — Die Zander'sche Gymnastik und das mechanisch-heilgymnastische Institut in Stockholm 1879.

— — Den Mekaniska Gymnastikens Apparelj och dess användning. Stockholm 1886.

— — Die Apparate für mechanische Heilgymnastik und deren Anwendung. Stockholm 1886.

— — Die Apparate für mechanisch-heilgymnastische Behandlung und deren Anwendung. Second enlarged edition. Stockholm 1889.

— — Om den habituella scoliosens behandling medels mekanisk gymnastik (On the treatment of habitual scoliosis by medico-mechanical gymnastics). Nord. Med. Archiv, Band XXI N:o 22, 1889.

— — Die Apparate für mechanisch-heilgymnastische Behandlung und deren Anwendung. Third illustrated edition. Stockholm 1890.

— — Die Apparate für mechanisch-heilgymnastische Behandlung und deren Anwendung. Fourth enlarged edition. Stockholm 1893.

Åberg, Dr. E. El Méthodo Zander de Gymnasia Mecánica. Stockholm 1884.

— — Resultados del Tratamiento obtenidos en el Instituto Terapéutico de Gymnasia Mecánica. Buenos Aires 1885.

— — Causas, Naturaleza y Tratamiento de la Scoliosis etc. Buenos Aires 1887.

— — Om användandet af »traitement forcé» vid skolios. (On the use of »forced treatment» in scoliosis). Extrait de »Hygiea». Stockholm 1893.

POSTSCRIPT.

While this book is printing we see that Dr. Zander's name has been ignominiously involved in some of the articles circulating in the European Press, relative to the »Electropathic» swindle of which the present proprietor of the Zander gymnastic apparatus in London has been accused. A few years ago this person unfortunately bought from a respectable English firm a set of Zander apparatus, delivered from Stockholm some years before to this firm, and placed them in his previously existing so-called »Electropathic Institute», engaging himself to practise the Zander method only under the supervision of medical men. But, according to what we have heard, he has chiefly been selling his »Electric Belts», carrying on gymnastic treatment to a very small extent, using it and Dr. Zander's name only as an allurement to a suffering public.

We need scarcely assert *that Dr. Zander and his method have absolutely nothing to do with this »Electropathic» swindle*, and we hope that the universal confidence hitherto shown the Zander method may not suffer by the conduct, in an entirely different domain, of the present owner of the Zander apparatus in London.

THE AUTHOR.

A 3.

Arm-pulling-downwards.

A 7.

Arm-rolling.

A 9.

Forearm-flexion.

B 4.

Hip-knee-extension.

B 7.

Velocipede-motion.

B 9.

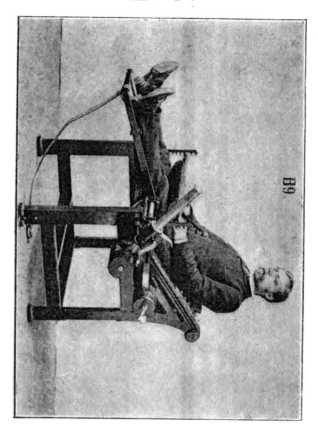

Knee-flexion.

B 12.

Foot-rolling.

C 5.

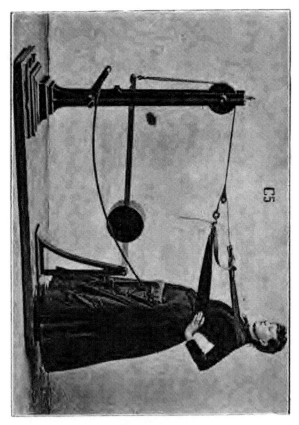

Trunk-extension (standing).

C 6.

Trunk-sideways-flexion.

E 6.

Chest-expansion.

F 1.

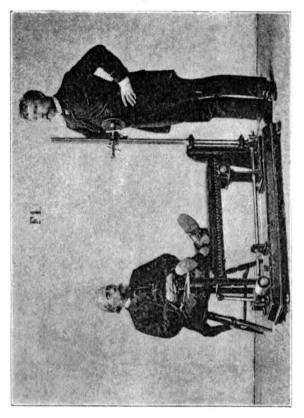

Vibration (of different parts of the body).

F 2.

Vibration, saddle-sitting, (of the whole body).

G 1.

Percussion (of different parts of the body).

J 1.

Arm-rubbing.

J 3.

Leg-rubbing.

J 6.

Circular abdomen-rubbing.

K 1.

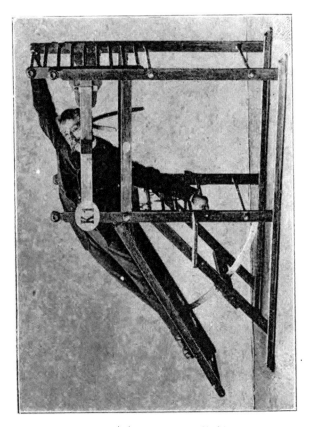

Lateral suspension (reclining).

K 2.

Lateral pressure (lying).

L 1.

Combination of A 3 and D 1.

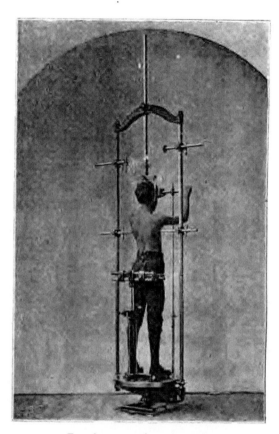

Trunk-measuring-apparatus.

THE MEDICO-MECHANICAL ZANDER

INSTITUTES

in Europe

● Fully equipped Institutes
● Partially equipped Institutes
● Single apparatus for private use
○ Institutes in course of foundation

out of Europe

● New-York, Buenos-Ayres
● Baltimore, St Louis
● Alexandria

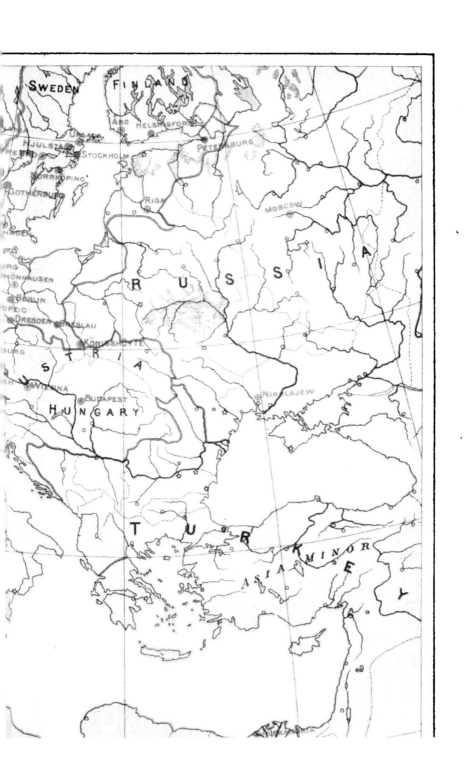

CPSIA information can be obtained at www.ICGtesting.com
Printed in the USA
BVOW02s1931270916

463460BV00018B/255/P

9 781166 024826